P9-CQN-382

My Girl

ALSO BY KAREN STABINER

Limited Engagements (a novel)

Courting Fame:
The Perilous Road to Women's Tennis Stardom

Inventing Desire: Inside Chiat/Day

To Dance with the Devil:
The New War on Breast Cancer

The Valentino Cookbook (with Piero Selvaggio)

All Girls:
Single-Sex Education and Why It Matters

My Girl

Adventures with a Teen in Training

Karen Stabiner

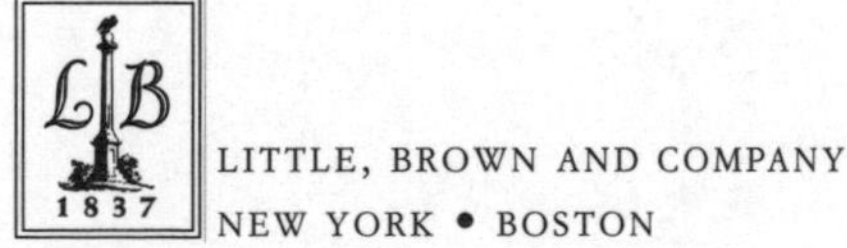
LITTLE, BROWN AND COMPANY
NEW YORK • BOSTON

LITTLE, BROWN AND COMPANY
TIME WARNER BOOK GROUP
1271 AVENUE OF THE AMERICAS, NEW YORK, NY 10020
VISIT OUR WEB SITE AT WWW.TWBOOKMARK.COM

FIRST EDITION: APRIL 2005

LIBRARY OF CONGRESS CATALOGING-IN-PUBLICATION DATA

STABINER, KAREN.
MY GIRL : ADVENTURES WITH A TEEN IN TRAINING / KAREN STABINER. — 1ST ED.
P. CM.
ISBN 0-316-60852-1
1. TEENAGE GIRLS — SOCIAL CONDITIONS — UNITED STATES. 2. TEENAGE GIRLS — ATTITUDES — UNITED STATES. 3. MOTHERS AND DAUGHTERS — UNITED STATES. I. TITLE.
HQ798.S726 2005
306.874'3 — DC22 2004016512

10 9 8 7 6 5 4 3 2 1

Q-FF

BOOK DESIGN BY MERYL SUSSMAN LEVAVI

PRINTED IN THE UNITED STATES OF AMERICA

For Sarah

"There are only two ways to live your life. One is as though nothing is a miracle. The other is as though everything is a miracle."

—ALBERT EINSTEIN

CONTENTS

PREFACE

IN THE FIRST DAYS OF PARENTHOOD, EVERYONE SAYS THE same thing: "Look at that." The slightest change is reason enough to drop what we're doing and watch. The baby smiles, the baby eats mashed carrots, the baby sits up or moves on her own. If we pay attention, a baby provides lots of opportunities for delight. We bore our friends and relatives, who are less stunned than we are by a new syllable that might conceivably mean "bird," but they tend to forgive us.

As a child enters adolescence, though, the inflection changes. "*Look* at that," we say, pointing to a muddle of discarded clothes on the bathroom floor. "Look at *that,*" we wail, wagging a finger at the retainer the dog has swiped for a toy. Preteens are too old to be entertaining merely by being alive and too young to be a reliable presence. We get impatient because they are suspended between two lives and we don't quite know what to expect of them.

That's when we start to worry about the next step. Within range of a driver's license, it may come down to one terse word — "Look."— a desperate attempt to get a teenager's wandering attention. How can we assert authority over someone who may well decide to ignore us?

If only it didn't happen that way.

My daughter, Sarah, was ten years old when I decided to write a book about our life together. I adored her — and yet the happier I was, the more mothers of older girls felt compelled to inform me that the end was near. We could not go on like this forever. They predicted that I would be miserable in direct proportion to my current state; if only we'd had less fun, those first ten years, I might have an easier go of it.

Worse, the nightmare would likely start earlier than it had in previous generations. Girls started to break away in the tween years, between ten and thirteen. A rebellious sixteen-year-old was a late bloomer.

I did not want to hear this. I sought out mothers I knew who had not voiced an opinion, mothers of older girls, and asked them if it was true: Was strife an essential ingredient of life with an adolescent?

Of course not, I heard over and over again. Of course not. I found women who had always loved being with their now sixteen- and nineteen- and twenty-eight-year-old daughters. They'd always been close. They dismissed the embattled caricature, and they apologized for not having spoken up sooner. They hadn't bothered to reassure me because they saw no reason for concern.

I talked to some of their daughters, too, in case the moms were guilty of self-deception. I got the same response, with a slight twist:

Not only did the girls value their relationships with their mothers, they were fairly sick of the prevailing notion that they must be, or have been, wretched adolescents.

Yes, everybody fought. Yes, mothers and daughters said things that they wished they could reel back in. But that was only a small, noisy corner of the larger truth. Somewhere along the way we had mistaken the occasional melodrama for reality.

I had told other people's stories for years. What if I watched us, instead? Or rather, what if I watched the next three years with the same appreciative eye that had made Sarah's first step such a memorable occasion? The happy mothers I knew had implied that there was a secret world behind the headlines and the outbursts, a satisfying place where mothers and their adolescent daughters lived most of the time. I might be able to find it, if I looked hard enough.

I was predisposed to believe them, because I wanted to and because the numbers were in their favor. There are about seventeen million girls between the ages of ten and seventeen in the United States. The most popular books on troubled girls are based on interviews with fewer than a thousand of them, all told. And these were not random samplings, which might have had statistical credibility: These were girls in therapy or girls who had responded to researchers' requests for subjects who had a particular problem; happy girls need not apply. One hundred percent of the sampling wanted to vent, or they couldn't be part of the sample — and yet we extrapolated from that small group to all adolescent girls.

Given the source of the data, assuming that all girls are troubled is like visiting Maine in December and assuming that the entire country is blanketed year-round with snow. It's not fair to the rest of the country; it's not fair to the girls.

So I set out to watch Sarah and her friends and to talk to some of the researchers whose work helped to define this generation of daughters. I listened to other mothers. I am not a sentimentalist, nor even much of an optimist, but I had to believe that there was more to the coming years than discord. I had heard rumors of happiness and thought that they deserved to have a voice. I set out to do what I had asked friends and relatives to do, endlessly, since the first time Sarah opened her eyes:

Look at that.

She was ten when I started and fourteen by the time I was done. My small sampling is no more statistically significant than all the bad-girl data, but it is no less true. In fact, our experience seems to match that of most mothers and daughters. The whole country is not frozen under a foot of snow, after all.

My Girl

1 Baby Love

CHILDREN GET YOUNGER RIGHT BEFORE THEY GO TO BED. Sarah is ten, all angles and bones, but when she is drowsy, wrapped in her flannel cocoon, she is six, maybe seven, flushed peach cheeks, soft curls, and a hazy grin. Back then she had light bones; I could hoist her in the air long after other kids her age were earthbound. Now I wonder how long it will be before I cannot carry her.

She says that if I pick her up every day I will always be able to, which makes sense so long as I do not dwell on it. I pick her up about once a week, but not the way I once did, scooping her up one armed, swinging her onto my shoulders, spinning her until I felt the centrifugal force tug at her wrists. I was loopy with affection; I could turn her upside down.

Tonight, lifting requires strategy and cooperation: She sits at the edge of my bed, wraps her arms around my neck and her legs around my waist, and on the count of three I step back and she holds on tight. My lower back complains, which it did not used to do, but we make it down the hall, Sarah squealing, "You can do it, Mommy," and I drop her backward on her bed.

She gets under the covers, I slide in next to her, and she tells me I should not go to New York tomorrow morning. We have this conversation every time I go, and I was wrong to think that it would get easier as she got older. Sarah clearly has inherited her father's high school debate-team gene and believes that she can talk me out of what I have to do. Resolved: There is nothing so compelling that it can come between us.

I say the same things I always say: lucky that I only go once in a while. Nice that daddy works at home. None of it makes a dent, and I don't blame her. Life is not a consolation prize. Lunch an hour from now is useless when a child is hungry, and almost home does not help if she is tired. Back on Tuesday means nothing when I will be gone for the six days between now and then.

I could act like leaving is no big deal and hope that she follows my lead, but who wants to raise a stoic? I pat the place where teachers still tell kids their hearts are. "You know," I say, "it's like me and my daddy. He's always with me here, even though he isn't around anymore. And I am always, always with you, no matter where I am."

That's good. Reassure her by bringing up a dead parent.

Luckily, she is too young to be morbid. For her, my father is shorthand for great parent, the kind of guy who still makes a strong impression twelve years after the cigarettes won.

"Mommy," she finally replies, "I would rather be with you forever than own a horse."

Sarah would rather have a horse than breathe.

"When I'm mad at you it won't feel that way," she goes on. "But it will still be true."

Mad at me? I was happy being better than a horse. I do not look forward to being the object of her scorn — and for the first time, I realize that there may be no way to avoid it.

A WOMAN I BARELY KNOW had come by a few weeks earlier to salvage my spindly rosebushes, a favor she dispatched with a quick display of five-leaf pruning and a stern lecture about horticultural neglect. Then she settled in for a cup of tea and the real fun, an unsolicited appraisal of my relationship with Sarah. I do not know her well enough to recall her teenage daughter's name, nor did she observe us long enough for her tea to grow cold, but that did not stop her. The specifics of our life were frankly beside the point. She had a universal truth to impart.

Life between a mother and a teenage girl gets as bad as it once was good, she said, and then, if the mother is fortunate, the girl takes off altogether.

This was not the first time I had been so warned. Women who said such things always had daughters who were old enough to drive, and their girls were rarely around when they made the prediction, having driven to the mall, the movie theater, a friend's house — the destination far less important to them than the ability to get there. They were elsewhere, which was all that mattered, while Sarah still wrapped herself around my shoulder like a vine.

The visiting mom seemed quite relieved to have been left in the dust, since lately being in the same room with her daughter involved a level of histrionics she found intolerable.

I meekly suggested that I would miss Sarah when she is grown up, but the older and wiser mom corrected me.

"No, no," she said. "Trust me. By the time she gets her license, you'll be thrilled to have her out of the house." Bereft, it seemed, was but a way station on the road to bliss.

She had no qualms about saying this in Sarah's presence, which struck me as unkind, like telling a child that the tooth fairy is a con. We were happy, even if it turned out to be temporary. Why did people want to tell us it would end? Because they were jealous, I told myself. I preferred this explanation to the alternative, which was that they were just like us, once, until adolescence made hash of their mutual affection.

Sarah was staunch in her defiance, probably because the woman's pronouncement scared her as much as it scared me. She clung to me ever more tightly and announced that it would not happen to us, and the other mother smiled a knowing smile and shot me a wink. I did not offer her a second cup of tea.

After she left, Sarah wondered how anyone could say such a thing. I shrugged. I told her I love her, which is my default position when I am confused.

My mother lives half the country away, and I do not recall much talk of love between us, but then, I had a more restrained childhood than Sarah does. In a midcentury midwestern suburb, we were big on proper behavior and suspicious of extremes of any kind. When my mother spoke of love, she did so with exasperation: It was a given in any good family, which was what we aspired to be, so there was no need to mention it. I suppose I am making up for lost time. I like to talk about love.

Bedtime always brings on the hyperbole. We can get a call-and-response going to rival a revival meeting. Sarah usually starts with a question, to signal that normal conversation has ceased:

You want to know something? she asks me.

What?

I love you.

I love you, too.

You're fabulous.

I think that about you, too.

We invoke infinity and endless galaxies, and then, when superlatives threaten to fail us, I bail us out with the same last line I have used since we started to do this.

"I love you more than words," I say, and she is satisfied. My husband, Larry, once asked if I meant that I love Sarah more than words can express or more than I love words.

Yes, I said.

The older she gets, the longer we go on, even on nights when I do not have a suitcase to pack. Mere mortals like the rose lady might fall by the wayside, but not us.

Or maybe we both know the truth, which is that someday she will want the car keys, and I will stay behind. Maybe we are shouting across the abyss.

THE ECONOMY DEPENDS on girls' having a hard time with adolescence, and on their parents having a hard time with them. If not for the hormonal tsunami known as puberty, there would be no market for parental-advice books, magazines that tell girls how to find a boyfriend and get their parents off their backs, fashions that change as quickly as a teenager's estrogen level, personal-care products to arrest or enhance the slightest deviation from the norm, or celebrities to mimic. Adolescence, the choppier the better, is a retailer's dream.

Parents are supposed to take on a new role when their children reach this turbulent age. The experts exhort us to be the anchor, the foundation; any bottom-loaded, inert object will do. The more mercurial our daughters become, the more grounded we are supposed to be. The mother who wants to be a pal to her girl is immature, self-indulgent, and in denial, and the mother who allows her own feelings to get in the way is shortsighted and irresponsible. The good mother should be firm and placid.

Like a concrete lake.

I'm sorry. The members of my family don't even sleep calmly. We consider tranquillity an altered state, little more than catatonia with a smile, and as such we do not expect to keep an even keel throughout dinner, let alone throughout a complete adolescence. I expect to vent as Sarah grows up, because venting was a second language in my parents' house — and because I have not forgotten how it feels for a blimpy little toddler to nestle in the curve of my neck, her warm breath making a steam spot on my skin. Growing up might be a new kind of fun, but it is still a good thing gone. There is an element of loss. Under the circumstances, I am skeptical, if slightly envious, of the perfectly composed.

I remind myself that this is not a tragedy. Tragedy is a forty-five-year-old kid who still lives at home, expects a homemade dinner every night, and never once offers to do the dishes. This is a comedy, in which a last-minute mom gets everything she ever dreamed of, familywise, and tries to hold back the hands of time because she is afraid of her daughter's inevitable adolescence — or rather, afraid of what people say about her daughter's adolescence. On any given morning, she wonders who will walk into the kitchen for breakfast, her daughter or her daughter's evil twin, and she wonders how she will let go, whoever it is.

I once worked with a woman who talked about emotion as though it registered on a Richter scale. Her goal was to stick to the midrange, where she felt safe, and she was prepared to sacrifice ecstasy, she said, if it meant she could avoid depression as well. Not me; no coward here. For a decade I have clambered the high peaks of motherhood like Heidi with her little goat. Now I wonder if I am doomed to fall as far in the other direction, in the name of some cosmic equilibrium.

SARAH'S FIRST TOOTH appeared on a TWA flight from Los Angeles to New York, and as soon as we got to the hotel I compromised her eyesight to get a close-up picture of her smiling mouth. Teeth were hardly a surprise, but they did mean that the pink-gum phase of her life was over. I did not want to forget it. We were still in the archival stage of parenthood, which included monthly so-big pictures of a naked baby set on a white blanket next to Larry's outstretched hand. In the context of new parents who have made one-hour photo labs a growth industry, I figured that first-tooth photos were pretty normal.

A few months later, she crawled across the living room and out of my line of sight, of her own free will. Until that exact moment, distance had been up to me. I left for work or had lunch with a friend; if Sarah went anywhere it was because Larry or I decided she should. But this time, she was the one who decided to split, and the only proof that she was still around was a maniacal giggle from the hallway, as she considered what she had done.

Things moved fast after that. We enrolled in a mommy-and-me program when she was two and a half, and for my pains I was rendered obsolete a year later, when she started preschool. She was so used to the building where we ate Goldfish crackers and drank juice that it was no big deal if I left her there, at least not for her.

It was not the kind of preschool I went to, where a stranger in a station wagon picked me up on the first day, and three hours later my mother had to borrow a car to retrieve her bewildered, weeping daughter, who was wedged behind an art easel and refused to come out. No, Sarah's preschool took separation issues seriously. Parents were on call for two weeks, until every last toddler was able to get out of the car alone. Our kids came home with masking-tape messages stuck to their shirts, and a big one, at the start, was "Mommy always comes back." It was hard to dig in the sand and finger paint, in those early days of independence, without the promise of Mommy to lean on at the end of an arduous morning of fun.

Nobody gave me anything to ease my side of the transition. I worked, but I felt like a slavering golden retriever; I lived to bring that bundle back home.

The last spring before kindergarten, I had to go to New York, so I bought five little white T-shirts and two fabric pens, and I designed a separation wardrobe for Sarah while she slept. She was reading by now, or memorizing passages in favorite books so that it sounded like she was reading. I wasn't always sure which, but I knew absolutely that there was one sentence she could read. Shirts one through four said, "Mommy always comes back," with a red X for each day that had passed. Shirt five added a new word and proclaimed, "Mommy comes back today!" Sarah politely stacked them in her drawer and refused to wear them. Who wants a T-shirt to commemorate loss?

It took me years to figure out that those shirts were for me. "Mommy always comes back" was potentially the cruelest hoax ever perpetrated on a bunch of three-year-olds, since who knows if anyone ever comes back from anywhere, but I needed to buy it wholesale if I was going to be able to walk out the door.

By the time kindergarten rolled around the following fall, I was smug enough about my separation technique to feel superior to the parents who simply dropped their kids off for the first day of school. I knew better. I milled around the yard with Sarah — for the record, I wasn't the only one — and when the kindergarten teacher asked everyone to line up, I dutifully took my place behind my only child. Then the teacher announced, "The parents can leave now, because we're going inside. We have work to do," and I stepped out of line. Elementary school had new rules of disengagement — and no, Sarah did not glance back at me as she marched into the building.

The stakes got higher after that. I have left Sarah at school, at friends' houses, at the bus for the annual out-of-town class trip. So what if I secretly rejoiced at her lack of interest in sleep-away camp? I took her where she needed to go, and I smiled and waved with the other adults. I am a high-functioning parent. I do what I am supposed to do, and nobody sees the effort.

ADOLESCENCE IS THE OLYMPICS of separation events; everything so far has been but a training program for the big developmental break, and I do not feel prepared. To my left, the worn road to embittered, the place where those mothers live who always wonder why you don't call more often, even when you call more often. To my right, the mysterious road to someplace better, for which the American Automobile Association has not yet published TripTiks. The rosebush mom was half right: Children do grow up and go away, and the pace in our household is about to pick up. I understand that big changes are coming. It is the pitched-battle part of her narrative that leaves me cold.

Sarah's childhood was such easy bliss, as I looked over my shoulder at its departing form. It was codependence at its finest. I was omnipotent and wise, she was needful and charming, and there was relatively little back talk. Daily life was full of the smallest of firsts — that bottom tooth, a scrupulously peeled inaugural apple wedge, the ringlet I had in a drawer someplace, an early *Sarah* written with a backward *r* — that were no less remarkable for being duplicated in billions of other households in the known universe.

It is hard to let go. Not chronic-depression hard. More like a squall: It hits and it passes. If I do a good job of being the mother of an adolescent, I guarantee myself only a temporarily broken heart. If I do a bad job, it could be much worse. I frankly haven't given much thought yet to what constitutes a good job in the next phase, but this business about her being mad at me someday got my attention.

I should be grateful for the early alert. Sarah is ten, a new tween — which, by the way, is what we called ourselves a lifetime ago, even though some millennial advertising type swears he invented the label and discovered the target audience. She is on the road to being a teenager. I have three years to get my act together.

IN NEWSROOM PARLANCE, If it bleeds, it leads. That is why the story about the teenage sniper runs at the opening of the newscast and the story about the altruistic students who tutor children with learning disabilities comes way after weather and sports. Stories about kids in between, the normal, run-of-the-mill ones, never run at all. We eat anguish for breakfast, and adolescent girls provide a lot of the fodder.

The public consensus is that they are a collective pain in the neck. They weigh far too little or far too much, they steal the car keys and the credit card, they lie through their orthodontured teeth about where they went and with whom, they hate themselves and their parents and the girls above or below them in the pecking order, and they think that oral sex is merely a southern-hemisphere version of a good-night kiss. They dress like tramps. They drink and smoke and spill booze and ash on the shoes they forgot to mention they were going to borrow. Their poor parents usually express helpless bewilderment, like folks who just watched a tornado take the roof off the house and hurl the pickup truck into the bedroom wall. Why, only yesterday, they say, my daughter looked like that sweet little cherub in the photo on the piano.

A causal link would at least provide a little comfort. A mom who fed her daughter junk food and never got her to school on time could speculate about the great girl she might have raised if only she had done a better job. Unfortunately, the commutative property does not seem to hold for child rearing: Stable girls have wretched moms, and troubled girls have pleasant moms, which means that even the best of intentions could lead straight to catastrophe.

Sarah may find ample reason to be angry at me as she gets older, whether I give her what I consider to be cause or not.

THE BOOKEND TO PUBERTY is menopause, which we have long believed would turn even Betty Crocker into Lady Macbeth, just as adolescence turns our lovely daughters into harridans. How scary is it? My internist began to lay the groundwork for hormone replacement therapy years in advance, making veiled comments at my annual physical about how much easier the aging process was for his patients on hormones, as though they stormed the office wild-eyed, wielding daggers, if they forgot to fill their prescriptions.

"Easier for whom?" I asked him once, and he chuckled and hit my knee with that little hammer.

He was wrong, as it turned out. Our worldview came from women who went to the doctor to complain about their menopausal symptoms, which was kind of like asking an agoraphobe how she liked the Grand Canyon. Nobody bothered to track down the women who were too busy enjoying life to drop by the doctor's office. When researchers finally did think to ask them, about two-thirds of menopausal women had no idea what the fuss was all about.

There it is. For a long time we thought that all women suffered, but we were wrong. Most of us lived outside the fray. What if most girls did, too? It might be that the girls who regarded hating their mothers as a team sport, and the girls with the kinds of problems that spawned headlines, were a vocal minority. Extrapolating from them to the population at large could set us up for calamities that will never happen.

What a glimmer of relief, just to consider the possibility. I imagined us happy when sixteen-year-old Sarah drove off in the car, and happy still when she returned. Happy through the process; unwilling to hate each other just for the sake of her growing up.

We would have to fight once in a while. As I recall, half the joy of shoes with decent heels was winning the battle with a mom who honestly believed that a nice pair of flats would not make you the target of instant ridicule. In my youth, everyone had to have at least one boyfriend her parents did not like and had to insist that any curfew was, by definition, an hour too early, just as any hemline was an inch too long. But those were episodic spats; anyone who has been married for more than a day knows her way around that kind of argument. What I wanted to avoid were the lingering, festering resentments.

That may not sound like much of a goal, but my family crest is anxiety rampant on a field of endless criticism. It would not be easy for me to get through the coming years without resorting to the dark parental arts — nagging, second-guessing, and the inducement of guilt.

MY FRIEND ANNETTE says it is possible. Annette has tremendous credibility because she is as unlike me as anyone of the same species and sex can be — tall, big boned, an observant Catholic possessed of a genuine faith, a serene presence — and since I am prone to self-doubt, I often embrace the voice of the admired Other as gospel. She and her husband have two exemplary sons, and I have sought her advice since the days when having a child was merely a topic for debate.

Some of what she did will not translate. I cannot support Sarah by making the predawn commute to swim practice, like Annette did with her older boy, because being a swim champ in our family means not drowning. I cannot befriend members of the religious bureaucracy, because I was force-fed piety as a child. I am not without skills of my own, though — I can bake desserts that make people want to invite us for dinner as long as I'll bring one, I know every Motown lyric worth remembering, and I can make up stories on the fly.

Does that make me a good enough mother to relinquish a daughter? "We raise them to go away from us," Annette once said, as though it were as simple a matter as making sure they had enough clean socks, "and if we do a good job, we make it easier for them when the time comes."

I was in awe. Unfortunately, I forgot to ask her how.

MY FRIEND CAROLYN says it is possible, too, having raised two daughters who not only love her but seek out her company. She did nothing as a parent that I care to emulate, as far as I can tell from her stories. If there was a rule in the parent handbook that she did not break, she cannot recall what it was. She is in no position to pontificate about child rearing, except that she survived two bouts of adolescence without any lasting scars.

She was appropriately cryptic when I asked her for advice.

"Rewrite the script," she said.

I was not intimidated. There may be no more arrogant hybrid than the baby-boomer journalist; there's the sense of entitlement that comes from being part of the largest population blip of the last hundred years, along with an urge to scour the earth for answers despite compelling evidence that they do not exist. In my lifetime, we have changed our attitudes about participation in foreign wars as well as about the benefits of whole milk, virgin brides, and foundation garments. I have witnessed a paradigm shift since I was Sarah's age. I am flexible and curious. Surely this qualifies me to survive her adolescence.

THE CAB HAS ARRIVED to take me to the airport, and the cabbie, wondering why a woman whose suitcase and coat are already in his car is still inside her house, has come to the door to see if I intend to join him anytime soon. Sarah, barely awake, squints at him with displaced resentment.

I sit down and she plops onto my lap. Sarah has always smelled to me like hot sand and driftwood, a wonderful dry smell that has nothing to do with people, and I have been known, over the years, to go back into her room to kiss her forehead long after she has fallen asleep, trying, in part, to memorize that scent. She smells that way right now. It has to go away someday, but it is not gone yet, she is not angry at me yet, and who knows if both those things will still be true when I get home.

I put my arms around her and start to sob. The cabbie retreats to flip the meter. We don't have to leave the curb at all, as long as I'm paying.

Like I said, it hits and it passes.

WHEN I GET TO MANHATTAN, I walk up to Central Park for a quick review of the carriage horses that have pulled the evening shift. I call home before I go to bed and tell Sarah about the good-looking white horse third from the front of the line. She tells me all about school and what Larry cooked for dinner. She hands the phone to him on the condition that she can talk to me again, and finally we run out of information to exchange. It is past her bedtime, and she has promised to get up early to walk the dog with Larry.

"Sweetheart, it's time to go to sleep," I say. "I'll talk to you tomorrow."

There is a sleepy silence.

"You could just put the phone on the bed and we could both go to sleep," she says. "Then we'd both be there in the morning."

"Sarah, it's really time for bed. You'll be tired tomorrow."

"Don't hang up, Mommy," she replies.

I don't, not right away.

2

Ten Going on Twenty

SUMMER IS MADE FOR SELF-DECEPTION. TIME IS LESS INSISTENT without school — is today Tuesday or Wednesday? — and there is more of it, so we get cocky. Sarah's biggest responsibility for the past twelve weeks had been to wear enough sunscreen and to remember to carry a water bottle. We watched old movies at odd times, and occasionally we broke media discipline altogether and ate dinner while we watched.

Now it was over. In two hours we had to show up at school for a traditional open house, to say hello to the teachers and see if last year's locker occupant left behind anything that grew. Tomorrow Sarah would begin sixth grade, her last year at her elementary school. In preparation, she had been in the shower for so long that the third person in the rotation could forget about hot water, singing so loudly that I heard her two rooms away: "Slap that bass, bada bada bada, slap that bass, slap away your trouble, learn to zoom, zoom, zoom — *slap that bass.*"

The fifth and sixth graders occupied the prestigious second floor, and all the kids knew to stick to the staircase closest to their classrooms. We followed Sarah as she headed up the sixth-grade stairs for the first time. Standing at the top, guarding the entrance to nirvana, were two girls Sarah has known since they were the smallest kids on the playground.

Over the summer they had acquired blond highlights, hairstyles that required not just a blow-dryer but the dexterous use of a round brush, and painted fingernails and toenails, the latter visible because they wore strappy platform sandals. Their tank tops were barely longer than a good sport bra, and they wore low-rise capri pants on their incipient hips.

They were eleven. One of them tilted her pelvis like a runway model and smiled a smile she may have seen in a magazine but had yet to grow into.

I thought about fleeing the country. I thought about calling their mothers to ask what the hell they were doing, allowing their little girls to look like that. Not that Sarah was spared appraising comments. Even with her limbs covered and her nails plain, people seemed to think that girls were put on this earth to be the object of public scrutiny. She did a decent impersonation of one of her admirers: "What big eyes," she cooed, rolling them toward the heavens. "What long eyelashes. What good posture." All true. Large slate gray eyes, ridiculous lashes, and the straight back of someone who would like to be taller soon. A broad forehead, and a mouth whose natural inclination is happiness, even in repose — full at the center, naturally tipped up at the corners. It is the same smile my mother wore in the photograph from my dad's college formal.

Sarah is slim and, for the moment, shorter than her friends. She has long hair that has not yet decided whether to be brown or very dark blond. My opinion of her appearance is properly suspect. When Sarah was a baby, she once threw up on me as our transcontinental flight took off, and all I could think, after I changed into a clean shirt, was how lovely she looked sleeping. But other people like the way she looks, too, so we have had to develop a point of view.

The man who sells bread at our farmers' market told Sarah recently that she could have a pretzel for free because she was so beautiful. The implication was that he would not have offered a pretzel to a plain girl. I had to wonder what he would have given Sarah if she had been dressed like the sixth-grade gatekeepers — an entire coffee cake?

I could not stop myself. "I'm having a pin made for her shirt," I told him. "It reads, 'I have a brain, too.'"

He handed her the pretzel, abashed. "Your mom is right," he said to her. "By the time you're my age nobody's gonna care how you look." He made a goofy face. She smiled.

A week later we bumped into a couple we know, and I got my first glimpse of their fabled sixteen-year-old daughter, who had Snow White's striking coloring without any of the chirpy facial expressions. I forgot myself and blurted out, "You are so beautiful," although I did stop short of offering her a free pretzel. Her mother, being six years ahead of me, had long since left righteous indignation behind.

"Inside," she said, with a conspirator's smile, "as well as out."

Oh, how I wished I had said that to the bread man. How I admired that mom, who saw a way to turn surface flattery into a lasting compliment. A girl who got a great roll of the genetic dice might as well enjoy it, but we live in a culture where women age faster than men do, and beauty too often gets mixed up with youth.

A parent can help. A parent can point out the more lasting qualities that a mere passerby might not notice.

I had tried to stay away from fashion altogether, so far, save a single edict that mattered only to those of us whose complexions lack pink tones: "Beige is not your friend." If the sixth-grade style twins were any indication, though, there would be thornier issues ahead, and I vowed to talk to Larry about a timetable for age at first manicure, age at first lipstick, age for pierced ears, for heels, for dates. I would not speculate beyond that. Sarah still thought that beautiful meant Katharine Hepburn in *The Philadelphia Story* or Grace Kelly in *To Catch a Thief.* When peer pressure kicked in — and I saw her give her friends the appraising eye — old movie footage might not hold up.

I mentioned various aspects of the teenage future to Larry that night, right before we went to bed. He responded with a look of complete bewilderment; I could not tell if the source of his confusion was the notion that Sarah would someday date or the cold realization that my X chromosomes were not encoded with the answers to such questions.

I KNEW ALL ABOUT the peer pack mentality. My junior high school friends and I always spent the waning weeks of summer looking for that must-have back-to-school fashion item. Every Saturday we took the bus to a nearby shopping center, and after an exhausting round of window-shopping, we retired to our favorite table at Edwards coffee shop for a round of strawberry ice-cream sodas and french fries.

Since we had far more time than money, we winnowed our desire down to a single, talismanic item. The summer before eighth grade, it was a slimy vinyl purse that hung in the window of a Chandler shoe store. I did not like the purse, which looked like a bowling ball crushed flat, but I had to have it, because the girls I wanted to hang out with had chosen it as the emblem of our friendship. My mother tried to convince me to get a red one instead, which only proved how out of it she was. No matter that I loved red and loved her. I spent $3.99 of my hard-earned baby-sitting money on the black one.

I had not thought about that purse since the day, halfway through eighth grade, when I quietly abandoned it, just as those girls would soon abandon me for being insufficiently cool. I supposed I would have to let Sarah buy the equivalent of a bad vinyl bag, if she should yearn for it, but not if it was as revealing as her friends' new tank tops.

How I would make sense of that contradiction — you may do what you want as long as it is what I want for you — was beyond me.

USA TODAY HAS CALLED today's teens the "richest generation ever." They spent ninety-four billion dollars of their own money in 1998 and forty-seven billion of their parents'; they influenced another three hundred billion dollars in family purchases by sighing loudly when Dad and Mom considered the wrong model car. Teenage girls spent thirty-seven billion dollars a year on clothing and about eight billion on health and beauty aids, and the reason they never had time to set the table was because they went shopping a minimum of once a week. One study swore the figure was as high as fifteen times a month.

All of this makes the slightly younger and more impressionable tweens a particularly delicious target for companies looking to establish brand loyalty — the kind of lifelong affiliation that makes soft drink manufacturers so eager to put vending machines in school cafeterias. Tweens are ripe for the picking because they wobble, as one marketer put it, "between childlike folly and advancing maturity." Loosely translated, they aren't sure who they are. They are willing to listen to any retailer with the right image to sell.

Just as a parent's credibility starts to fade, the booming voice of marketing says, Own this particular item and you will be cool. The other girls chime in. If parents are not careful, what used to sound like personal taste might soon sound like a dinosaur chorus.

ON THE FIRST MORNING of school, Sarah stood against the dining room wall for her annual photograph. When she was in the second grade, an overzealous housepainter covered over our penciled hash marks before we could stop him, so we depended on these pictures to show us how she had grown. This year she was taller than the light switch, which had not been true on the first day of fifth grade.

"You're going to be taller than me," I said, not for the first time but with a new certainty.

She insisted that she would not, even though she knew I was right. The first day of sixth grade was change enough, for now.

We got into my smug little mom car — the four-door, box-shaped, safety-enriched Volvo sedan I would have bet my life I would never own, the one that made hip single people (like I once was) snicker when I pulled up next to them with a backseat full of girls. It had taken me months to convince myself that my own personal brand identity would survive a Volvo, and yet at the moment — the car smelling of newly sharpened pencils, plastic binders, and spin-dried clothes — all I wanted to be was the mom.

When we got to school, we forgot ourselves and started up the fifth-grade stairs out of habit. Halfway up, Sarah realized her mistake and turned to head back down.

"We're going up the wrong stairs," she said.

"But there's a hall upstairs you can go across," I said, failing to grasp that her very identity was at stake.

"*Mom,*" she said.

I was chastened.

Why not get the red purse.

Mom.

We walked across the playground to the sixth-grade staircase, where she stopped.

"Want me to go up with you?" I asked.

"No, that's okay."

And she was gone. Just like that.

IF PEOPLE NEEDED a justifiable reason to be in a funk, there would be fewer of us taking Zoloft or Prozac. Members of my parents' generation, the ones who survived uppercase bad news — the Depression, World War II — doubtless consider my generation to be emotional hypochondriacs, frantic over the psychological equivalent of a hangnail, medicated to blunt the sharp edge of life being less than perfect. I have an alternate theory. Perhaps all those years of encounter groups and trust exercises have paid off, and we are simply more in touch with our feelings than our ancestors were.

However you look at it, the big blues of my day were that my daughter had begun her last year of elementary school. I could have been pleased to have a morning to myself, but I focused instead on what I didn't have — Sarah to talk to, and anyone else to listen to me complain. Yes, Larry was in his basement office, but I tried to respect the separation of church and state and not bring my personal issues into his work space, at least not while he was sitting at the computer or on the phone.

I was by myself in a rather profound way, since most of my best friends did not have any children. One could not, one thought she wanted to and changed her mind, one never found a man with whom to share her life, let alone collaborate on a new one. Carolyn had two daughters, but they had left home long ago, and her two grandsons were older than Sarah. She had already put in her time; I felt guilty when I went on too long about motherhood.

I would not call my newer friends, three women whom I have known since our girls started kindergarten, because I refused to be the wimp of the quartet. They were probably thinking the same thing.

Instead I paced, which irritated the dog, whose herding instinct required her to follow me every time I left my office. I walked into the empty room where Sarah did her homework, I wandered into the kitchen, I walked to the head of the basement stairs and waved silently to Larry, in case he felt like taking a break. He waved back and didn't budge. I tried to will the phone to ring, which would absolve me of any moral responsibility. If someone called and asked how I was, I could hardly be faulted for telling the truth.

It worked. I told my mother how hard the morning was, in great and unnecessary detail. I marveled at how fast the summer had gone. She, of all people, would understand what I was going through; Norma had sent two of us off to college, and we never lived in the same city again. She knew the pain of separation.

She replied, "The older you are, the faster time moves." That's how joyous my family's outlook was: If I thought today was hard, it was only going to get worse, and quickly; by the time my mom and I hung up, Sarah would probably be driving. Norma neatly excised the part of the cliché where people at least get to have fun while time flies. In our family we just stood there, growing wrinkles and losing muscle mass, as life howled by.

So I changed the subject, and after a few more minutes of chat, I announced that it was time to go back to work. Self-pity always defers to pragmatism in our house, since we are a two-income family, like most couples with children in this country. Privilege was not something we were born with, like the trust funders, nor did we grasp early enough that there were ways writers could achieve it, most of them having to do with writing fewer words per page and using terms like *close up* or *cut to.* Investment luck? Canaries in a coal mine had a brighter future. We bought our life one project at a time and felt grateful to have the chance. We were like the guy I once saw on television who spun plates atop long sticks: very impressive as long as he kept moving.

Work was one of the things I would still have when Sarah grew up and had a life of her own. Larry, our mutual health holding, was the other. And my friends — the childless ones for sure, since we had already weathered my defection to the other side, and, I hoped, the situational friends, the school moms. It would be just like before Sarah was born.

No, not just like. Teens get all the attention, because puberty is such a developmental apocalypse, but along the way there is another, more subtle truth. My mom friends and I will be different, too, when we arrive on separation's opposite shore, when Sarah has her own zip code and a couch we wish she'd thought about twice.

WE NEVER INTENDED to have a child. I met Larry when he was an editor at a magazine staffed by people who were either too cool to have children or too cool to talk about them, a place where staffers were warned that spending too little on their expense accounts made everyone else look bad. He was talented, tall, funny in an arch kind of way, not bald, had an elegant nose, and knew more history than I had studied in my lifetime. He had a wall of record albums, he had already weaned himself from televised sports, and his glance promised passion, not domesticity.

With time, a few less-endearing attributes emerged — the man refused to dance — but by then we were so in love that we could tolerate the occasional disappointment. Life was going to be one long, fascinating, adults-only dinner party.

The first time I saw him in the same room with a toddler, the kid was trolling for fun and Larry was pressed up against the wall, hoping to be mistaken for an armoire. I was equally uninterested. I was a wretched aunt to my niece and nephew — not that I was aggressively bad, just that I failed to acknowledge their existence for months on end. Children belonged to people with another agenda.

Then my dog and my father died within six weeks of each other, and suddenly the family landscape was down to a smaller oasis and a lot of drifting sand. That dog was my first pet out of college, the one constant in two cities, four houses, and a couple of fried relationships. My father was the one emotional slob in a family full of tacticians. I thought of myself as a cool character, but in the backwash of a bad month, a strange new idea came to me: My family had fallen apart, and Larry and I could make a new one.

But first, we had to talk it over. The U.S. National Center for Health Statistics said in a 2001 report that the number of births to women over thirty-five had more than doubled since 1980. Social pundits had a very good time discussing the reasons for the trend, from a woman's desire to establish herself in the workplace to medical advances that stretched her childbearing years into what used to be grandparent territory. They missed the obvious: We were not a generation known for its spontaneity; from the sexual revolution to protests against the Vietnam War, we liked to be part of a movement, preferably one that ran counter to received wisdom about how to behave.

Women are supposed to have babies in their twenties.

Says who?

My being thirty-eight was not the issue; habit was. We were not sure that daily life would expand to accommodate a baby, so we talked, endlessly, aimlessly. After months of debate, I decided that any decision was preferable to more conversation. I took out two sheets of paper, wrote Pro and Con across the top of each one, drew a line down the center, and instructed Larry to come back in a half hour with his list. I went into another room and did the same. The results were almost identical: The pros were romantic, and the cons were environmental screed. Love carried the day.

And then nothing happened. As our future failed to materialize, month after month, we retreated to our corners. Larry insisted that we would continue to have a wonderful life as an eternal duet. I just as fervently insisted that we would not. After a year we gave up on the ovulation kit and the calendar and went back to thinking of sex as a recreation, not a strategy. I got pregnant immediately.

To make sure that I got my full measure of deferred enjoyment, I stayed pregnant two weeks past my due date. The obstetrician, who used the euphemism "premium baby" rather than ask me why we had waited so long, decided to induce labor. There would be no middle-of-the-night hospital run for us. We got ready for childbirth the way we prepared for a long plane ride: We showered and washed our hair, put on comfortable clothes, packed up the *New York Times Magazine* crossword puzzle and a couple of pencils, and headed for the hospital.

Twelve uneventful hours later, the doctor announced that he needed to perform a C-section, though in my cold disappointment I wondered if he was motivated by my lack of progress or by his dinner waiting on the table at home. I wanted the pain, the sweaty profanities, the ecstasy. I did not want a procedure.

"Only if you get it done right away," I replied, as though I could choose to come back and try another day.

Sarah was born thirty-eight minutes later. The doctor explained that she had been stuck because her chin was not tucked down the way it was supposed to be.

"She is looking up at the world," he said, trying to put a positive spin on an epidural and stitches. I bought it. In the days that followed, Larry and I turned bad birth-canal presentation into a life view. Sarah was curious, Sarah was eager, Sarah was raring to go. Of course her chin was up. There was so much to see.

What an unremarkable trio we were, two gawking parents and a ruddy, shut-eyed little bawler in a peach-colored, hospital-issue cap and booties. Almost four million children were born in the United States that year. It didn't take any particular skill, beyond failing to use birth control; lots of things took more effort and more time, like becoming a doctor or learning to fly.

But look at this: two people and a new life. With luck, and given the actuarial odds, I would know Sarah from the first moment of her life until the last one of mine. I have known my sister since the day she came home from the hospital, but I was not yet three, not impressed by the gravity of the occasion. I have known Larry for almost twenty years, but I still feel cheated for having missed the college years, or his early days as a magazine writer. Falling in love as an adult depends a lot on hearsay, which is never as reliable as being there. Sarah was my one and only chance to see a life unfold.

I had spent my working life scribbling in steno notebooks and taping interviews, looking for a story — but no matter how copious the notes, I never, ever got everything. It wasn't possible; I came into people's lives in the middle. Not this time. I was greedy for information on Sarah, the brand-new person. I wanted us to go out for tea when I am ninety.

For that matter, I wanted to go up the sixth-grade stairs with her on the first day of school.

* * *

AT DINNER SARAH COMPLAINED that an irritating new teacher's aide found it hard to believe that Sarah was in the sixth grade. "You're so small," Sarah reported her saying. "I thought you were in the fourth or fifth grade."

"I'm sure she was just trying to make contact," I said, already plotting to have her fired. "But it wasn't a very considerate thing to say."

Even I hated the way that sounded.

"How about saying this to her?" I said. "Hey, you're so dumb I thought you were younger."

Sarah laughed in astonishment.

"That's exactly what Daddy said," she replied.

She tried out various snotty retorts and decided on the one she liked the best.

"I may be small," she cried, "but my brain takes up most of my body!"

The next day she came home enraged. This was not the vague "mad at you" that she had mentioned last spring. No, right now she hated me. I had called the curriculum director at school to rat out the teacher's aide, but in an excess of care, it came back around to Sarah. One of the teachers took her aside to discuss how she felt about what had happened. She felt ambushed, is how. Worse, she was insulted that I had intervened.

"I shouldn't say this," she said, fairly vibrating, "but it was *stupid* of you to say anything."

That was the last thing she said to me for an eternity or two. I went into my office and paid bills. I shuffled papers. Finally, well into the next century, she appeared in the doorway.

"Where's Daddy?"

"Running errands."

Five minutes later she came back.

"When's dinner?"

"Stephanie's coming." Sarah would undoubtedly convince the baby-sitter to have the locks changed.

"She is?"

"Yes. You two can figure out what you want to do for dinner."

Five more minutes, and a third appearance.

"Mommy?"

"Yes?"

"I'm hungry. What is there to eat?"

A tiny opening.

"Can I make you something?"

"Yes."

It is hard to find a way back when someone is that angry, but reheated pasta can fix almost anything. While Sarah ate, I apologized for what was an error in judgment on my part; I should have told her what I was going to do or else not done it. I had not expected anyone to talk to her, and I had learned a lesson. I hoped that this would not affect her coming to me to talk things over in the future.

"No," she said. "Well, it did when I got home."

She should have been asleep by the time we returned from the movie, but when we got out of the car, I looked up at her bedroom window, counted "One . . . two . . . three," and the blinds cracked open. She was lying there in the dark, waiting for a kiss good night. I was forgiven.

For what? I tried to protect her, which was exactly what I had done since the day I found out I was pregnant and gave up coffee for a hideous hot grain beverage, gave up alcohol for water, and gave up chocolate lest her metabolism be disturbed by the caffeine in a single M & M. I saved her from things she did not even know about, from the drunk who caromed toward her little umbrella stroller to the dental hygienist with a heavy hand.

It is my job to take care of her, but she is in sixth grade now, and today I stepped over a line that used to be three feet to the left.

The Transitional Mom

IF A COUNTRY CAN HAVE AN ID, LOS ANGELES IS IT: WE DO what other people want to do or work hard to deny that they want to do or pass laws to keep themselves from doing. Balmy outside, balmy inside. If you want a stern superego, try Chicago. Los Angeles wants me to relax and try new things.

So I admit that I go to an acupuncturist, which seemed a reasonable alternative to three dermatologists who could not banish a simple rash on my upper arm. I liked her the moment I met her. She was born with a forgettable American name like Judy, and in a spasm of self-actualization changed it to something that sounded to me like a menu item at an Indian restaurant. She wore batik without apology, and she played world music on her office sound system.

She got rid of the rash. After that I went to see her every couple of months, just to keep my energy pathways open, which I considered not half as goofy as people who took growth hormones to turn back the hands of time.

I kept an appointment in late September even though I had a massive head cold, for she swore that the needles worked best in a crisis. I sniffled and listed my concerns, which included not just clogged sinuses but Sarah's middle school applications, whether Larry would make good on his pledge to cook dinner two nights a week, and how long I could survive with no free time at all — the endemic, unresolvable litany that made working mothers one big encounter group.

Why I said this to a woman who had no spouse and no children, I do not know, but I would take empathy wherever I could find it. Silently she inserted her little needles along an ancient road map, a process as comforting as it was mysterious. When she finished, she offered up her diagnosis.

"Your whole problem," she said, kindly, "is that all your ch'i is in your head." She placed the side of her hand against her throat, passed it over her face, and tapped her forehead. "Up here. Not good."

"What should I do?"

"You have to get the ch'i flowing down into your feet," she said, "through your body. Do something with your feet. Take a walk. Don't think about everything so much."

FROM WHAT MY RELATIVES TOLD ME, I was born thinking, a serious, sensitive little brunette who arrived a month early and complained strenuously about the eviction. Many of my childhood photographs can only be described as solemn. I got my schoolwork done on time. I was never rumpled. Even so, my parents wrung their hands a lot.

When I was well past thirty, I found out that they had had a premature baby before me, a boy who lived just long enough to get a name, and suddenly all the careful fussing made awful sense. They knew something a parent was not supposed to know — that there is no sure way to keep a child safe — but the futility only made them work harder. It seemed as if they held their breath around me, and I became cautious to spare them concern.

Only the people who lived on the route where I walked our dog knew of my lush secret life: I could sing any tune from *The King and I, Oklahoma!* or *The Sound of Music,* and I did, at the top of my nine-year-old lungs, while I stood in the dim morning light and pried lumps of snow from between Duke's pads. When I got older I taught little girls to fingerpick "Blowin' in the Wind" on the guitar, insisting that they learn every single verse. I had a one-night job singing in a restaurant, until the owner decided that an electric band would be a better draw.

And yet Larry never heard me sing until Sarah was born. I grew up in a house with rules set as close together as pilings, and so I found it hard to let loose in front of people I cared about.

With Sarah it was different. Someone had to teach her the Motown canon and some rhythm and blues. Inside the Volvo, I sang "Locomotion" along with Little Eva, as loudly as possible, and Sarah danced in her seat while I pounded out the rhythm on the steering wheel. Inside the Volvo, we sang along with Sam and Dave, and Sam Cooke, and Martha and the Vandellas; that was our car rocking back and forth at the red light. Between us there was no such thing as foolish behavior. She called me "weird," and I knew it was a compliment.

I did not think about how I sounded. Like the little me on a walk with the dog, temporarily sprung from expectation, I did not think at all.

As a mom, I was bold from the very start; one of the things I liked best about Sarah's early years was that I did not have to be responsible. Yes, I enforced crossing at the light and not licking the plate, but beyond that, reality was no concern of mine. For years I was a blithe guest in the endless elsewhere of childhood.

And then it began to change, bit by bit. I could dig my heels in as hard as I liked, but Sarah and her friends would go to a new school for seventh grade, one that took them all the way to high school graduation. There would be grades, tests, classes on how to take those tests, and ever more homework, all in the name of a bright adult future. It was our job to figure out what school was likeliest to point her in the right direction, which first required us to figure out which direction that was. It was time to contemplate what came next.

I studied the private school brochures and applications, and what brought me up short were the photographs of the eager, intelligent, ambitious, athletic, well-rounded, and appropriately diverse young people. They seemed so focused. They fastened their gaze on a distant horizon; they had a goal and a way to get there. The brochures said that Sarah could develop a passion for calculus, for ancient civilization, for Advanced Placement Latin, for track. School would send her into the world with a sense of purpose, and we were supposed to want this badly enough to pay for it. The entire educational-industrial complex, the test-preparation classes, the tutors and private coaches, would crumble if not for this desire. The yearning was nothing new, but the fever pitch was unsettling.

We lived only three zip codes away from people who imported elephants for their children's birthday parties. On this side of town, private school was hardly considered an indulgence, but for us it was still a tricky decision. I went to a big public high school and survived, thanks, and I feared that private school would make Sarah a snob, more comfortable at elephant birthdays than in an entry-level job. Larry had always felt he was odd man out at the old-money private school his parents had scrimped to send him to; not a lot of good memories there. On the other hand, there were no public schools in our neighborhood like the ones I went to, so that was a rather empty exercise in politically correct nostalgia.

We could work harder and make the private school tuition bill, and we could deal with whatever the teen prestige equivalent of elephants was. My real fear was that a college-prep school would make good on its promise and catapult Sarah so far from home that we would hear from her only on birthdays and holidays — and along with the rest of the television audience, perhaps, when the evening news interviewed her about her landmark legal victory against Big Tobacco.

Or she might be catapulted and land with a resounding thud. Everyone knew some perfectly splendid person who never quite found the proper niche.

Or every single school might turn her down, depriving us altogether of the luxury of this kind of worry.

Or, or, or. Overthinking is the curse of the adolescent's mom. Freud may have puzzled over the question of what women want, but that is nothing compared with the question of what women want for their daughters. Specifically, what does a hardworking postfeminist want for a daughter whose horizons are as broad as the Montana sky? I was in constant, clandestine dialogue with myself about how to give Sarah a great life, whatever that was.

She might have a very different definition than we did. I once asked Larry what he would do if Sarah fell in love with a politically conservative Mormon who raised minks for a living, which was as far away from the familiar as my imagination would take me, short of scenarios that involved felonies. I didn't really expect her to do so, or she might and he'd turn out to be a swell guy, but right now that prospect symbolized life outside our comfort zone. What if that was who she brought home, a decade or two from now?

"If she loves him," he said, "I don't think there's anything I can do. As long as he's not an ax murderer. Or a polygamist. Is there?"

No.

All of this in the fifteen minutes I spent needled up on the acupuncturist's table listening to musicians imitate the sounds of gulls and crashing ocean waves. I could have meditated if I knew how, or I could have taken a nap, but my brain refused to let me go. Ch'i in the feet was not going to be easy.

I WAS NOT THE ONLY ONE who had the bad habit of looking ahead. At dinner Sarah reported that her math teacher had offered to create a seventh grade, for one student, so that Sarah could stay at her current school for one more year. Sarah could choose a friend to keep with her, and if no one else wanted to stick around, the math teacher would be her friend. They could have lunch together every Friday.

Sixth grade was barely under way, and the math teacher was already in mourning.

"That is so sweet," I said. "Did it make you want to cry?"

"No," she said, suspiciously. "Are you starting to cry?"

"No. I'm going to save all my tears for graduation." I began to bawl — loud, fake sobs — and Sarah laughed.

"I'll have to stop my speech in the middle," she said, referring to the sixty seconds each child got to sum up publicly his or her feelings about elementary school. "'I'm so glad to be done with sixth grade'—'Mom, could you please be quiet?'"

Having imagined the possibility, she was concerned. "Are you going to cry all through my speech?"

"No," I said. "I'll start crying the minute you walk through the door. I'll try to be quiet during the speech."

Somewhere I read that we make two distinct kinds of tears, the ones that accompany physical pain or distress, and the deeper ones, impossible to control, that flow from the heart. I was frequently ambushed by the second kind. All of those early attempts to civilize me did not quite take.

SARAH AND JULIA liked to remind both sets of parents that they knew each other before we did. They met at six months, when their respective child-care people struck up a conversation on the sidewalk, but Larry and I didn't meet Julia's mom and dad for at least another six months after that. The girls were now the oldest of friends, and they found all sorts of opportunities to hang out. Julia was a semiregular guest for Tuesday-night dinner, since her parents worked late and being with the baby-sitter wasn't the fun it once was. Beyond that, the newest excuse for coming over was the study date, which the girls knew would impress their academically ambitious parents. They set up shop in the spare bedroom at Sarah's desk, a wooden door on top of a couple of file cabinets, and vowed, virtuously, to do all their homework together.

They did, briefly. Or they pretended to. Then they snuck into the living room, and somehow a Beatles CD got turned up too loud for anyone to concentrate on anything but the music. Just as I thought about lowering the volume, the girls shot through the doorway on rolling desk chairs. They careened through the living room like pinballs, barely missing the couch and a glass table. They pushed with their feet, lurched around in circles, and sang along at the top of their lungs. Then they turned off the music and disappeared, just as quickly. I went back to washing lettuce. The only sound emanating from the front of the house, now, was the assiduous scratching of a couple of number two pencils.

SIXTH GRADE was supposed to be about independence, in anticipation of the rigors of middle school. Time management was a big deal, so the kids got overlapping nightly assignments and weekly assignments and even assignments that were due at the end of the month. Sarah had to learn to shoulder these responsibilities, and we were supposed to support her effort.

Larry embraced a wait-and-see stance; he was around if Sarah had a question, but he was prepared to read the paper or answer e-mails if she didn't. He waited for her to take the initiative.

I didn't. I nagged.

Nagging is the developmental stage right before obsolescence, the death rattle of the reasonable mother, and if I kept it up Sarah would learn not to talk to or hear me at all. This did not stop me. One month into the school year, I had become the mother from hell, the one who reminded Sarah to finish her homework two minutes before she was going to do so. My timing was impeccable — no matter when she intended to do something, I got there first to ask why she had not.

Even as I spoke, I stepped outside my body and listened to myself in horror. The principal, the teachers, the talking heads who came to parent association meetings, all said the same thing: You have to let your children make mistakes; you have to help them become independent; better they should forget their homework and face the consequences than depend on you to remind them.

In other words, lay off.

Of course, they simultaneously wanted me to make absolutely sure that Sarah's school record was pristine, her life laced with so many extracurricular activities that I passed myself on the street as I drove from one to the next.

I got it. I must be sure not to do everything for her — but while I was at it, I better do everything for her.

She responded by dragging her feet ever so slightly, not enough to get into trouble at school, just enough to let me know that she resented the meddling. One afternoon, when I was being a particularly rigorous pest, she ate an after-school snack in slow motion, as though daring me to tell her to hurry up. She lolled through the half hour we should have spent at the dog park. When she did get around to her homework, she took offense that I had to cook dinner instead of keeping her company.

Called to the dinner table, Sarah announced that she was not really hungry, not after that big snack. Besides, she had to finish the homework I had been after her to finish. Was I suggesting that she ignore it?

Got me there.

Larry, meanwhile, had collapsed on the couch after a three-day work siege and had promptly fallen asleep.

The dog looked up at me and wagged her tail, in case I needed someone to help me eat what had been perfectly cooked clams. I dropped a couple of them into her dish, since three minutes of neglect had turned them into little rubber pellets, and then I was seized by the urgent need to get out of the kitchen and off by myself. I had pestered my child until she turned on me, and assigned way too much significance to Larry's exhaustion (so which is it? Bored with me or with my cooking?). I shoved the rest of the food to the back of the stove, where the dog could not reach it, and tromped upstairs to our bedroom. If I could have gotten away from me, I would have. Short of that, I could at least spare my family.

I was one sarcastic comment away from an entire evening of arch silence, and I did not trust myself to go back downstairs until I calmed down. Yes, today was a stressful day, but no worse than any day that began with an off-center ponytail and ended with a belligerent child and some overcooked seafood. I had to learn to handle that level of tension or I was going to be in big trouble when we moved up to dating and a driver's license.

MY MOTHER LEFT US ONCE. We didn't see it coming. There we were, on a Sunday afternoon — my father eating Italian cherry peppers out of the jar, my sister at the Betty Crocker play kitchen making cake that bounced, me making a tile trivet with watery glue that dripped everywhere and was fun to peel off my fingers once it dried. My father was known to burp to make us laugh, and my sister and I sometimes forgot and pushed our hair behind our ears without first washing the cake mix or glue off our fingers. My mother was a preternaturally busy woman. That kind of aimless fun, which wouldn't include her until we reached the cleanup phase, probably got on her nerves.

What a self-absorbed trio we were, deaf to her entreaties about not leaving a mess. At the time, I blocked out most of her requests, since I had entered the phase where anything I was repeatedly asked to do was, by definition, not worth doing. My younger sister tended to follow my lead, and my father, at the helm of a family restaurant-supply business that had not lived up to anyone's expectations, was simply too tired to care.

So she walked out on us. I remember it as though it were a movie. It was summer. She had on a turquoise sleeveless blouse and matching capri pants, and she wore her hair in a cap-coif called a bubble. She swept down the short hall of our house with her purse and a sweater over her arm, grabbed the car keys off the kitchen table, and headed for the Chevy Malibu.

I stood at the open kitchen door for a moment, paralyzed. As she pulled away from the curb, I ran into the middle of the street and yelled, "Mom," over and over, fully expecting her to stop dead as soon as she remembered that she had children.

She kept driving. I ran into the house and confronted my father. "Where did she go?" I wasn't so much frightened as I was put out. How inconvenient, for a mother to behave in such an unpredictable fashion.

He was flummoxed. "I don't know."

The three of us stood there for a moment, considering the likely consequences of her departure, which included starvation, no clean underwear, clothes in puddles where we left them, an inexorable descent into a feral existence.

A quick search of the house revealed that the icon of personal hygiene had left without a toothbrush or a washcloth. She could not be going far. We called Aunt Junie, who was not related by blood but had known my mother since college. It was a good guess. Junie said that they were having coffee and that my mom would come home in an hour or two. Which she did, to the most attentive, obedient, appreciative husband and daughters a woman could ask for, at least until we forgot and reverted to normal.

We had her back where we wanted her — dishing up Rice Krispies and orange juice every morning, feeding the dog I forgot to feed, reminding my sister to brush her hair, emptying my dad's ashtray. Her life would have been enough to send me over to Junie's for eternity.

* * *

I HAD NO IDEA what the last straw was, that day. Had she folded one too many pairs of socks? Was she hoping that one of us would notice her hairdo or make the bed without being asked? No idea, none whatsoever. I could have asked, or she could have said, but she was by then invisible to me. We had stopped talking about anything but logistics.

Sarah undoubtedly had no idea why I was upstairs; for all I knew, she considered herself lucky that I was. I had started this mess, and I would have to stop it. I made myself go back downstairs. I woke up Larry, I apologized to Sarah, and we shuffled into the kitchen, a humbled trio, for a makeshift meal.

WHAT IF PARENTHOOD were like any other job and involved application, evaluation, and possible rejection? It is the only major endeavor in our adult lives for which we need no qualifications; even marriage usually involves a protracted period in which each party assesses each other's merits. We regularly dismiss potential spouses for having too many old flames or too few prospects. We are far more forgiving about who reproduces.

The collective résumé is not impressive. If I were hiring, I would say first off that a prospective parent should be dependable — and yet this generation has a 50 percent failure rate on marriage, our only other lifetime job. We seem to have a fatal tendency to misjudge people.

A parent ought to be practical, too, since someone has to make sense of a world where every kid wants her own four-hundred-dollar personal music system. But we have hardly proven ourselves to be fiscally responsible. Simply put, we don't save money — though I suppose we can hope for children who do, as their act of rebellion, and then ask them for a loan.

As for consistency, forget it. The national personality suffers from a rather severe bipolar disorder, spending $40 billion on diet aids each year to help us shed the weight we gained spending $116 billion on fast food. If we took all the weight lost on yo-yo diets over the last ten years, we'd probably have enough excess poundage to build another planet.

Fickle, self-indulgent, and completely lacking in discipline: If children were handed out on the basis of parental merit, it might be much easier to achieve zero population growth.

Ah, but we are a clever bunch, as adept at denying responsibility as the people who keep us waiting in line at the post office or the bank. Like any incompetent faced with the consequences of his incompetence, we deflect the blame onto the only people around who have less status than we do — our kids.

IN 1993 CULTURAL HISTORIAN Barbara Whitehead published an essay in the *Atlantic Monthly* with the incendiary title "Dan Quayle Was Right," a reference to the vice president's complaint about Murphy Brown, a sitcom character who decided to become a single mother. Whitehead said everything that the progressive modern-day parent did not want to hear, which boiled down to this: Of course our kids are a mess; in the name of our own happiness, we've robbed them of the stability they need for theirs. Divorce pulls the rug out from under our children, whether it leads to single parenthood, sequential romances, or remarriage. Whitehead didn't come out and say that people ought to stay together for the sake of the kids, a popular notion when I was growing up, but she did line up statistics and let people draw their own conclusion — which was that children from intact families seem to get along better in life.

Five years later, Judith Rich Harris published *The Nurture Assumption: Why Children Turn Out the Way They Do,* a book that attempted to retire forever the notion of a parent's omnipotence. Harris analyzed the existing research on families and came to a startling conclusion: Beyond the genetic legacy of their DNA, parents have little influence on how a child turns out. An intact family is a perk, no doubt about it, but hardly the deal breaker.

Peers make kids who they are, and if a child falls in with a wrong crowd, there is little if anything parents can do about it. They might not even realize what has happened. There is no way to elicit information if a girl prefers not to provide it, no way to demand obedience if a girl feels compelled to pierce her tongue or experiment with drugs, no way to get her to do homework at the computer when instant messages are so much more fun. Much of the time, parents don't even know enough to argue, since they've been told that all the frantic keyboarding is a paper on *Romeo and Juliet* for English class.

According to Harris, parents who insist that they know who their daughters are, and what they're up to, are only proving how gullible they are. A clever girl figures out how to behave to keep her parents at bay. When they are in the audience, she acts the way they want her to act, and the rest of the time she is her true self, which might be completely different. It seems that we are missing an important category at Oscar time: best performance by an adolescent girl in an enduringly deceptive role.

Whitehead said that parents set the stage for trouble. Harris said that parents stood in the wings while trouble happened. I could behave as though my actions mattered and face eternal self-blame if life with Sarah somehow turned sour, or I could stand on the sidelines and pray that she sought out a nice set of peers. I opted for action, however futile it might turn out to be. At least I'd have something to keep me busy while I waited for the story to spin itself out.

MY MOM PALS at Sarah's school must have been front-row girls in their day, like me — the ones who sat right under the teacher's nose and always raised their hands, the ones who took copious notes and did the extra-credit problems. The other kids might have considered us a pain in the neck, but we didn't care. We knew that smart was the ticket out and anonymity was no prize, so we spoke up whenever we could.

Aside from our shared curiosity, we were an unlikely quartet, with little in common beyond our kids. There was Lori, my mentor as a kindergarten room parent and the only friend I had who didn't work; Julia's mom, Phyllis, from up the street, a clinical psychologist out of a Catholic school; and Jo Ann, a self-made marketing executive for an oil company.

At the first parent association meeting of the school year, Sarah's principal saw the four of us sitting together, and I could swear I heard the smallest sigh escape her lips. She could depend on us to ask questions, and follow-up questions, and to approach her after the meeting had adjourned. The four of us always spurred each other on.

She passed around a handout entitled "The Journey through Adolescence," and with it died any hope of easy answers. It turned out that adolescence was not one stage but four — emerging adolescence, early adolescence, late adolescence, and transitional adolescence — starting at age eight and culminating at "22 . . ." Anyone who had ever used an ellipsis knew what those dots meant: The author wasn't making any promises about an end to the turmoil at twenty-two. For that matter, the principal explained, each child experienced the stages differently, sooner or later, quicker or faster, sometimes overlapping.

Adolescence was like fingerprints: Everyone had them, but no two were the same. We thought we had to survive only the teen years, but in fact the siege lasted far longer than that — fourteen years, minimum. It was, said the handout, a passage "through unprecedented physical, social, emotional and intellectual change."

The principal, a valiant developmentalist, looked up from her notes at three dozen paralyzed faces. She smiled. "They'll come back," she said, "and that's the good news. My girls are in their twenties, and I can promise you, they'll come back."

The smile turned wistful. "But they'll be different when they do," she said. "It will never be like this again."

LARRY DID SOME SPEECHWRITING WORK for an out-of-town company, and when his clients came to Los Angeles, they wanted to go out to dinner. By the time we finished the entrée, I knew as much about automotive safety as my mother must have known, in her day, about my father's restaurant-equipment business.

It will never be like this again.

Sshhh.

Around 9:30 I pulled a long maternal face and apologized. We had told our friends that we would pick up Sarah by ten, so I had to leave. Larry could stay. It was lovely meeting all of them.

A half dozen people flipped their cell phones in my direction and, as one, instructed me to call to say we would be just a little bit late.

I was trapped. I felt the same way I had on our first night out, six weeks after Sarah was born, when we had just enough time between feedings to catch a movie. We did not have time to stand on the wrong level of a multilevel garage while Larry searched futilely for our car and I chanted, with ever-increasing urgency, "I have to get home. I have to get home. *I want to go home right now.*" These nice people merely wanted to uphold capitalism and make sure I got to order dessert, but it was all I could do not to upend the table and bolt out the door.

THERE IS NOTHING as boring as other people's travel photographs. We have sat, half-asleep, and forgotten on purpose to keep our fingers on the white borders, in the hope that our host would snatch away the remaining photos — and then we have imposed the same tyranny on our friends. I have tortured people with pictures of everything that mattered to me in Italy, sometimes multiple shots of the same meaningful place, from overlapping perspectives.

Why do we do this?

Because we want to believe that we exist beyond the limitations of our circumstances, because we want to believe that self is not a function of situation, and because we fear it is not so. We want witnesses who see what we see in those pictures — that the inner adventurer has survived the constraints of daily life. That there is more to me than a harried commuter between car pool and desk.

We were planning a family trip to Italy for the coming summer. We went whenever we had enough frequent-flyer miles to make it only marginally crazy, as opposed to flat-out nuts; I liked to remind my skeptical mother that aside from the plane fare it was no more expensive than Disneyland, and the ice cream was better. We went despite friends who wondered what could possibly be left to see, although they had been married to the same spouses for a decade or two and felt no compelling need to find new and surprising ones.

When it was time to trade the miles for tickets, I told Larry that I would like to spend an extra week alone with Sarah. I was away seven times last year, for work, and I envied him that time with her.

Besides, if the doomsayers were right and teenage girls all came to hate their mothers, then I wanted one last fling before she turned on me. Not time stolen from daily life but a whole week without intrusion, no phone, no fax, no e-mail, no deadline — a journey away from here, however brief.

Sure, he said. He had missed something, too, over the past year: a single day without responsibilities. He could spend a week staying up too late and eating dinner while he watched a baseball game. Working dads needed a break, too.

I asked Sarah if she was interested, and she said yes.

We took our first trip to Italy the summer before kindergarten, and in the weeks before we left, I sent Sarah letters from Rosetta, the bilingual cousin of her favorite stuffed bear, who promised to be waiting for us when we got to the apartment we had rented in Florence. A friend's older daughter sneered at the obvious deceit, but Sarah walked into that apartment expecting to find Rosetta, which she did, because I had darted into the bedroom and planted a stuffed bear on the table next to her bed.

Sarah's faith in magic was confirmed; anything could happen, because it did. I wanted a piece of that back before she got old enough to have doubts. I wanted memories to stockpile, material for the next generation of little girls who wanted to hear about Rosetta the Italian bilingual writing bear. I saw myself as an old woman, surrounded by eager young relatives who considered me a rapturous storyteller. I knew plenty of made-up stories, but I told them true ones whenever I could, for I had always loved stories that just so happened to be real. They always began with the same phrase: And then, there was the time.

I TOLD MY MOTHER about the Italy trip, and she asked if she could join Sarah and me for that last week.

If I said yes, I lost my time alone with Sarah.

If I said no, then someday Sarah would turn me down when I wanted to go to Italy with her and her daughter, and I would feel what my mother was probably feeling: disappointed, left out, marginalized.

So I feinted. I reminded my mother that we had already invited her and her second husband to join us for one of the weeks when Larry was still there, and she replied that it was pointless to come all that way for one week. She wanted two weeks, one of which would be alone with me and Sarah.

What if they met up with another couple for the second week instead?

Her husband did not really like to travel in the summer.

So she wouldn't go for one week, but he wouldn't go for two. I tried again. What if she and a lady friend spent a second week in Venice? I could work any number of permutations, but it was senseless. She wanted me to invite her. I was not even sure that she was eager to go, but she wanted to be asked. I took a deep breath and said no.

Five minutes later I called back to explain myself. I wanted one week when all I had to do was be with Sarah. I didn't want to be responsible for anybody else's good time.

"It's not going to be long before Sarah doesn't want to spend every minute with me," I said.

"Tell me about it," she said, and gave up.

The timing was so bad: Out of fifty-two weeks in a year, my mom wanted me to be part of her life for the one week when I wanted Sarah to be part of mine. I was sorry, but I couldn't yield. I wanted a good, long glimpse of Sarah while I still had the chance, and besides, there were all those perfectly good options my mom had refused to accept.

For every action, there is an equal and opposite reaction. A mother cannot stand still when a child pushes off; something gives way, and I hope it will be my common sense and not my nerve. A generation from now, I have to be ready to go to Italy even if Sarah does not invite me — with Larry, with a friend, by myself. I do not want to start coming up with reasons not to do things.

4 Matters of Life and Death

I IMMEDIATELY SIGNED UP FOR AN ITALIAN CLASS, AND ON the first night, I got to the Italian Cultural Institute fifteen minutes early, plenty of time to find a parking space anywhere but Los Angeles. On my fourth fruitless lap, I felt the finger of defeat tap me on the shoulder: You're going to be late; you should have left earlier; you weren't ready in time to leave earlier; you may as well not bother. There must be something useful you should be doing.

As a freshman in college, I got lost on the way to my sociology seminar, and instead of asking for help I sat down on the nearest bench and cried. I would not give up again. I drove three blocks and paid the kind of parking lot ransom that Los Angeles drivers have come to expect, and then I ran all the way back to the institute.

In my mind's eye, I had imagined making the kind of entrance denied to those of us who have so often settled for clean instead of well-groomed; I would be the handsome woman of a certain age and just a touch of mystery who glided to a seat at the far end of the front row. Instead, I lurched to an empty chair and almost disemboweled myself on the desk arm. I landed loudly, sweaty and flustered, the strap of my shoulder bag pinning me to the chair like a seat belt.

This was supposed to be one of those cool independent things I would start to do as Sarah grew up and asserted her autonomy, but all I did in the first five minutes of my new life was disrupt everyone else's. I was determined to catch up, so I became the student everyone loved to hate. I wrote down everything the teacher put up on the board. I whispered the answers to all the questions, even when he called on someone else. I worked so hard that my teeth ached by the time the two-hour class was over.

When I left I could tell any Italian I met that I have a black dog whose name is Bella. *Io ho una cagna nera qui si chiama Bella.* That should be a great conversational icebreaker next summer, by which time I might even be able to add that Sarah found her on a pet-rescue Web site last fall.

WHEN I GOT HOME I went into Sarah's room to kiss her good night, even though she was already asleep. It was awfully dark. I wondered, When did we stop turning on the night-light?

We would have given it up long ago if it had been a generic night-light from the hardware store, but it was a foot-tall crescent moon that emitted a cool, silvery glow, a gift from her self-appointed godfather, Harry, and an essential part of the evening landscape. At the start she wanted it on because it provided safe reference in the middle of the night; later she called me back to turn it on so that she could have one more hug and kiss.

I could not remember the last time I did that. In the last month or so, Sarah must have stopped asking, I had forgotten, and now it was part of the past, along with shoes that were as wide as they were long. And leggings, which as recently as last year were the garment of choice at Sarah's school. They came in purple and fuchsia and giddy flowered red velour, but when she grew out of them she chose jeans and chinos, in more sedate denim and tan. I could not say exactly when she made the switch.

No lamp, no leggings. Even "Mommy" had faded into the dim fringes of the day, right before she fell asleep and right after she woke up. The rest of the time, she used the more restrained "Mom."

I was not so much sad as I was astonished; I thought I was paying attention, and yet the night-light had slipped right by me. I fell into bed, muttering the conjugations for *essere,* "to be," wondering what other markers had passed without my noticing, wondering what else I might want to do besides speak Italian.

SARAH LIKED JOHN, though they were separated by eighty years and a good two and a half feet. When she was eight, we went to a reading of his stories about life as the son of a Presbyterian missionary in Shanghai, and at intermission I announced that it was past her bedtime, on a school night, and time to go home. She replied that she was not tired and would be fine tomorrow. Then she marched back into the auditorium to take her front-row seat without waiting for me to respond.

To keep from fidgeting, she took paper and pen out of my purse and began to draw — first one of my earrings, and then the shoes of the women in the front row. A tiny enamel heart with a rose at the center, followed by a pump, a sandal, a flat, and a platform with straps.

We stayed until the end. We had the drawings matted and framed. Sarah presented them to John the next time we were together, and he bent his gaunt frame into a question mark so that Sarah could see close up how pleased he was to receive them.

She liked John's story about being a Boy Scout in China. She liked to listen to him read at our Passover seder, in his sonorous, professorial bass. We always gave him the longest passages, and he never shirked — no matter that he was a missionary's son. John and Carolyn had lived together since long before I knew her, she was my friend, and faith was faith, whatever the denomination, so they showed up, and they read. Each year, Sarah got a little braver about approaching him. She asked for a copy of a children's book he had written, and then she asked for more, autographed, please, for her best friends. She liked John, and he liked her back.

And then, just like that, we never saw him again. His heart was no longer up to the task of going out much, so he stayed at home more and more, and then he died. Over a hundred of us gathered on the lawn behind Carolyn's daughter's house for — not a funeral, not even a memorial service, with its implied piety — an event about John. His daughter, a rangy woman in her vague fifties or sixties, stepped to the podium and sang the song he always sang on car trips. His grandson did not even have to open his mouth to make people smile, since he stood exactly the way John did, one shoulder forward and slightly dipped, his hand gripping the front of the podium with an entitled air.

Carolyn's younger daughter and son-in-law read from "The Empty Box Haiku," a series of fourteen poems that John had written to cheer a faculty colleague whose empty office mailbox had come to symbolize a greater void. The whole lawn shimmied with laughter at each one:

The empty box
Makes space in its corners
For tomorrow's letters.

And,

The clean lines
Of the empty box
Teach perspective.

And last,

Tomorrow is today,
Fulfilling
The empty box.

When Carolyn's older daughter spoke, I wrapped my arms around Sarah, and she did not wriggle away. Carolyn did not speak to the crowd at all.

The family put copies of John's writings on a table in the front hall for us to take on our way out, which they hoped would not be for a while. There were tables to sit at with strangers who wanted to tell their favorite John story to someone new, and there was an endless Chinese buffet. Desserts and coffee were inside the house. We ended up talking to a woman who had had a crush on John before I was born.

By the time we got to the little table, all of the books were gone, except for one small, gray booklet of poems. Sarah grabbed it, hesitated, and put it back, worried about taking the only book left. Carolyn saw her do it and hurried over to hand the book back to her.

"John would want you to have it," she said.

Emboldened, Sarah confessed that what she really wanted was a copy of the empty box haiku. Carolyn promised to get that one for her, too.

Then she returned to her post at the front door, where she spoke to her friends as they left. When Sarah got there, Carolyn dipped slightly — she had less distance to cover than John did — held out her hand, and said how glad she was that Sarah had come.

Although I stood right behind Sarah, I had the eerie feeling that they were far away from me, that I was witness to a moment in her life that had nothing to do with whose daughter she was.

There is no one as grave as a girl who has a large emotion to express.

"I was glad to be here," Sarah said, a short lifetime of affection in her voice.

WELCOME TO EVENING OFFICE HOURS. Sleep experts say that unstable hormones precipitate the kind of insomnia that wakes women up after their first deep sleep cycle, around three in the morning, but it is the day's unfinished business that keeps us awake. The frantic pace of most women's lives fails to allow for the downtime we need to get our mental house in order. Unable to attain peace during waking hours, we try again while the rest of the family is asleep.

The night after John's party, I had to wrestle mortality before I could hope to return to dreamland. Someday I would expire, and what drove me absolutely nuts was that I would miss the mundane events of Sarah's life on the following day. I do not believe in the hereafter — but even if there is an afterlife, I doubt that it provides tracking information on beloved relatives. I have spent my working life looking for truth in the telling detail. My private hell is any place where I do not know what is going on.

And that, after all, is motherhood: a process of ever-increasing ignorance, culminating in being rather permanently out of the loop. We start walking on water; we end up at best a lovely reminiscence. I have begun to regard young women with a new suspicion: I have to resist the urge to accost the random twenty-five-year-old and ask, Have you called your mother today? Does she know about your new haircut, new project at work, new boyfriend?

Probably not. I never thought that she should, when I was on the daughter side of the equation.

I WAS NOT ASLEEP YET.

Marika was my dog before Bella, and she was already an old lady by the time Larry and I got married. When her ancient back legs gave out, the kindly veterinarian offered to drive over to our house on his way home to administer the shot that would end her life. I sat with her under the kitchen table to wait for him, because that was where she liked to sit and because I could not bear to be far away from her for the ten minutes we had left together.

I stroked her head and told her how much I loved her. Then I moved around in front of her, so that she could see I was serious, and I whispered, "Listen. If there is someplace else after this, save me a spot."

The vet was quite discreet. He waited across the room until I beckoned to him, and then he waited with the syringe until I nodded permission. I bent over and muttered, "Good dog, what a good dog you are," until she couldn't hear me anymore, and then he put her in a big black plastic leaf bag and took her away.

I thought about not telling my parents, but now that my father was too ill to go to the office he called every day, and he always asked how the dog was. If the dog could have talked, I suppose she would have inquired after my dad.

So I told him that Marika was dead, and he said he was sorry.

"She had a beautiful life," he said.

"Yep," I said, "a wonderful life."

"No," he said, with a note of asperity. "It was a *beautiful* life."

I had no idea why he insisted on the distinction.

My father's name was Ira. Sarah's middle name is Ivria, after him, and they have certain things in common. Ira was all about motion. He loved to ice-skate; we hung on to his speed skates for years after he died, just to be able to glance at them and remember him slicing across the ice. He was always ready for a horseback ride on summer vacation, or a game of tennis or a round of golf. There is a home movie of my parents when they were very young, my mom standing up to her ankles in ocean, my dad swimming out, coming back, swimming out, coming back, trying to get my mom to go with him, to no avail. After his funeral, back at the house, my mom and some of her friends took out the old movies, and I found out that the swimming movie was made right after their first baby died, and their parents sent them to Florida for a rest. That explained why my mother looked so blue and why my dad kept urging her to swim. He was not one for sitting still.

Funny, how inheritance works. I never thought of myself as athletic; I saw myself as more my mom's girl. And yet now I was the parent in motion. Like most kids, Sarah wanted to ride bikes and ponies, to roller-skate and ice-skate, too. She had no siblings to play with, and Larry avoided any athletic activity that required balance, having had a bad childhood experience with a bicycle and a banked driveway, so she turned to me for company. She dismissed the warnings of the sideline moms and told me to put on my skates, to canter around the ring, to come on in, the water's fine. I acquired an array of protective gear and told the voice of reason to shut up. I was my father's daughter, as it turned out: I had forgotten how good I was on skates, and I was game for everything else.

I was head over heels with the Sure! Why not? of childhood, and grateful to get back some of what I had had with my dad.

A couple of weeks ago, I reminded Sarah of the conversation my dad and I had had when my old dog died, to make a point about how two people could use different words to describe the same thing. Or maybe I was still searching for an explanation, since I never really understood what Ira meant. She looked at me as though I had forgotten how to speak English.

"A wonderful life is one that's so perfect nothing ever goes wrong, and that isn't even real and it isn't going anywhere, so who would want it," she said, in the instructional tone I had just used to explain the new electric toothbrush. "A beautiful life is, with everything that goes on, it's still very good. That's the kind of life your dog had. That's the best kind of life anyone could have, since the world is never perfect."

Looking for Trouble

SO WHAT.

A middle-aged, middle-class woman dotes on her daughter and tries to figure out what it means to be a good mom. How average can we get? My family has so far failed to produce any alcoholics, practicing or recovered; drug addicts; child abusers or victims of abuse; prescription junkies; the morbidly overweight or underweight; anyone but serial monogamists. No May–December romances, no gay people, no enduring romantic relationships outside the faith. No Nobel Prize winners or elected officials, and not a single guru, corporate or otherwise. No arrests, not even for a misdemeanor. We always remember to vote.

We prefer our dogs and our cars midsize to large, but we reject SUVs on safety and environmental grounds. We like well-made clothes that last, for we understand that the more urgent a trend, the quicker it will disappear. I own shoes that are older than Sarah — but you'd never know it, I take such good care of them.

My dark brown hair is my own, as are the dozen strands of gray.

Larry and I have used the same baby-sitter, once a week on Fridays, since Sarah was five.

Anyone still awake?

I live a life I did not even bother to ridicule when I was younger, since disdain would have required me to acknowledge it. We are a comfy nuclear family.

We ought to be smug as cats. A psychologist I interviewed, years ago, explained what he called the "downward comparison": We are drawn to stories about people who are worse off than we are, he said, because it makes us feel better about our own situation. He was talking about cancer patients, who collected other people's bad news like planks of wood and built a little platform of optimism. As long as they were not at the bottom of the prognostic heap, they felt better. They had hope.

The dynamic doesn't quite hold for parents, though — as it turns out, economic health and domestic stability are no guarantee of a peaceful adolescence. In fact, the irony of families like ours is that we have bought our kids the chance to get into new kinds of trouble. Lyn Mikel Brown and Carol Gilligan studied one hundred upper-middle-class students at a private girls' school in Ohio for their 1992 book, *Meeting at the Crossroads: Women's Psychology and Girls' Development,* and they found girls whose self-esteem spiraled downward at the onset of puberty, even though they had every comfort to buoy their spirits.

Brown has continued to study the emotional lives of adolescent girls, particularly the sources of their anger, so I sought her out, in the hope that she could explain the connection between external comfort and internal distress — or better still, that she would say it was exaggerated out of all proportion to reality. The notion of a girl who had everything but happiness was a painful one to parents who had hoped to provide opportunity, not alienation. I would feel much better if Brown said that she had met plenty of carefree girls who belonged to our demographic slice.

She had, but not enough to make a mom sleep easy. According to Brown, happiness can predispose an adolescent to unhappiness — girls who are safe from overt dangers like poverty simply find other ways to get into trouble. "Sometimes problems are more subtle simply because they can be," Brown told me. "If you are a middle-class girl and you have your needs met, if you have enough food to eat, for example, then you can use food for what it represents — power and control."

Poor girls faced problems finishing high school, a higher teen pregnancy and birth rate, and an environment of drugs and violence that made a walk with that new baby into a dangerous enterprise. More fortunate girls danced their own sorry two-step: Parents who could afford health insurance had daughters who could afford drugs; families with plenty to eat had daughters who consumed too much or too little; those of us with access to birth control had girls who thought that abstinence was for nuns. Society had a dark sense of humor. Many children who should have had the sunniest of lives ended up depressed, wishing for an indefinable something that they did not have.

A year after Gilligan and Brown introduced readers to their unhappy subjects, psychologist Mary Pipher recounted her experience as a therapist to troubled adolescent girls in *Reviving Ophelia.* That book and its offshoots (*Surviving Ophelia, Ophelia Speaks,* and more) quickly became indispensable parenting tools, right up there with disposable diapers and juice boxes.

Along the way, all those stories of adolescent casualties achieved critical mass; they became not information but a belief. Teenage girls lose their self-esteem, and that is that. Teenage girls indulge in one self-destructive behavior after another. "Difficult teenage girls" is a redundancy, since there seemed to be no other kind. Any girl who says she is fine probably lacks sufficient self-awareness to understand her plight.

It pained Brown to hear that kind of talk, since it was never her intention to imply that girls are, by definition, a mess. Yes, they have to separate from their parents, and yes, it can be hard to do, but that was no reason to write off the next generation. She and Gilligan had hoped to illuminate our daughters' lives so that we might better understand the process of growing up. They had intended their work as an aid, not a condemnation. Brown bemoaned the "generalizations" about adolescent girls that we had come to accept — and she was haunted by the memory of a colleague who approached her at a psychology conference and said, "We're still recovering from the misunderstanding" that had grown out of her work.

"To a certain degree, there's a caricature out there now," she said, "and girls get really tired of hearing that they're going to have low self-esteem, they're going to have bad relationships with their moms, they're going to have abusive relationships with a boy. It's not that simple."

Parents too often took the most minor emotional skirmish as proof of the coming thermonuclear war; we were so worried about our daughters that we failed to notice the days when nothing much was wrong. Parental concern had gotten out of hand — instead of making the girls' lives better, our assumptions had polarized us even further.

Life might improve if we stopped expecting the worst. Scare statistics looked a lot different when I turned them upside down:

Ninety-seven percent of girls do not have a diagnosable eating disorder.

Eighty-five percent of girls have no issues with food at all.

Only 15 percent of children between six and nineteen are overweight, as opposed to one-third of their parents.

More than 85 percent of teenage girls do not get pregnant each year.

The rate of teenage intercourse has decreased every year for the last ten, even though age at first intercourse has continued to drop as well.

Illicit drug use is down among teenagers, who have managed to do a better job of just saying no than their parents have.

Alcohol use is "unacceptably high" among teens — 18 percent, according to one government study. But the same study claimed that over half of all Americans had reported "current use of alcohol," so we might want to reconsider that predinner cocktail before we start complaining about the kids.

Two and a half million girls participate in high school sports, up from three hundred thousand in the 1970s.

More women than men attend and receive degrees from four-year colleges, and the number receiving advanced degrees is growing.

I was no Pollyanna. I intended to be vigilant until Sarah was out of the woods, at thirty-five, maybe forty. But Brown had suggested an appealing alternative take on life — that we had unfairly condemned our daughters, inflating anecdote until it became cliché.

ON MY SIDE of the family, we carried our anxiety in our hands: ring-twisters, nail-biters, handwringers. My father finally gave up biting his nails after his college poker pals teased him about it, substituting a lifelong commitment to fastidious nail care. My mother adjusts her rings and kneads her arthritic fingers. I stopped shredding my cuticles in a lover's pact with Larry, who simultaneously gave up Coca-Cola, but my hands were always looking for something to do — baking, braiding Sarah's hair, a fast game of gin rummy.

As we pulled up in front of a prospective new school for a visit, I noticed that Sarah worried at her fingers, as though they might flutter if she did not hold them in place. She was hardly the only one feeling apprehensive. One girl walked by tugging her ponytail tight enough to stop her circulation, while another walked an embarrassed three steps in front of her mother, who refused to stop talking about whatever it was that the girl did not want to hear. An open house, alongside every other family that might apply to this school for seventh grade, was not an easy way to spend a Saturday morning. These were the dark days when even the most doting parent privately worked the odds with an uncharacteristically cold and calculating eye.

We sent Sarah to an elementary school where they didn't give grades and rarely gave tests. Now people she did not know were going to judge her, along with hundreds of other children whose parents loved them as much as we did Sarah, based on an interview, a letter from the principal, school records, and a couple of standardized tests. Someone — many someones — would be disappointed. I had not felt this protective since the baby-sitter tried to take Sarah out for junk food.

Larry huddled with his dad pals, taking refuge in a debate about city politics, but the front-row moms took silent measure of the other parents and of the girls huddled with their elementary school pals. There were two things at stake for us: We wanted the girls to go to a wonderful school, and we wanted all four families to end up in the same place.

People make fun of suburbs like the one where I grew up, on the outskirts of Chicago, and they have a point — those neighborhoods were as homogenized as milk. But they had a continuity going for them that I long for now. The families on my childhood block moved into the neighborhood when their kids started nursery school and moved out, every last one of them, when we went to college. For fifteen dependable years we caught fireflies, raced our bicycles, and shoveled snowy sidewalks for fifty cents, together. My parents had their Saturday Night Club, eight couples they'd known since their college days, my unofficial aunts and uncles. For decades they got together on the first Saturday night of the month and on all major holidays; they paid witness to each other's lives.

I wanted something like that, more than I would have imagined. I loved the idea that sisterless Sarah would have three friends who could say, "We grew up together," and that Larry and I would have friends who recalled everything about our children since their kindergarten production of *Peter Pan.*

The faculty members cut the herd like seasoned cowpokes, parents sent to the auditorium and girls somewhere else, and as they passed, I heard one of the two girls who were hanging on Sarah's arm say to her, "Don't let me get lost." Sarah had attended summer school here a year ago, and she knew where things were. She had a job to do; no need to knit her fingers.

By the time we caught sight of her again, she was sitting at an outdoor table making Halloween cards for a community service project. I veered away from our tour group — not enough to embarrass her, just enough to make voice contact — but when I said hello she barely acknowledged me.

She fit right in.

What did my mother say? *The older you are, the faster time moves.*

* * *

THE PARADOX OF MODERN LIFE is that the following sounds like nothing: We drove two cars to the school open house so that I could go directly from there to Italian class and Larry could take Sarah home to do homework while he packed for a business trip. Two hours later he brought her back to me on his way to the airport so that I could drive her to a drama class.

Our life felt more than busy to me, and yet we knew people who raised a baffled eyebrow at the opportunities we allowed Sarah to miss. We had not sent her to an intensive academic-enrichment summer program; in fact, when we did send her to summer school that one year, it was with express instructions to avoid all academic classes. She took cooking and drama and swimming. We were not interested in accelerated sports programs at nearby universities. Occasionally I advanced the antiquated notion of free time and watched other parents' eyes glaze over.

The words "we allowed Sarah to miss" were theirs, not ours. The unspoken follow-up question was, "Don't you want her to get into Harvard?," which was code for, Don't you want her to be the best? The immigrant creed of always wanting more for your children was a noble one, but it could get crazy when the parents in question already had plenty of everything. Our generation was engaged in an extracurricular feeding frenzy: The biggest mistake a modern parent could make, it seemed, was to utter the word "Enough."

Some children seem happy leading polyphasic lives, like miniature CEOs, and it is not worth debating whether this is pure joy or an acquired taste. I'm all for activity, up to a point. What makes me squirm is strategy, the cobbling together of an impressive résumé for a kid who might secretly yearn to do something else, or nothing at all.

We could fill every waking moment with activity — work! culture! friends! and in southern California, the imperative of frequent exercise — or we could just be. I picked up Sarah at five o'clock and considered her slightly wilted form.

"I think we need pizza and a movie," I said, and she looked relieved.

I doubt that knowing a whole lot about old screwball comedies will do much for her school applications, but there it is. We have already blown it: We said no, thank you, to the brainy-kid camp, complete with its sample SAT, and we plunked her down on a pony, when more pragmatic parents would have nudged her toward a recruitable collegiate sport like soccer or basketball.

We pulled out the bed tray that was a wedding present from Carolyn and John, got into our pajamas, and ate our pizza while we watched the movie. When Sarah is older, she may remember the times that she and Larry and I spent together with no goal but being together, which has to matter as much to a sixth grader as a premature but highly gifted appreciation of medieval literature.

Cake

I ALWAYS CRIED AT MY BIRTHDAY PARTIES. FOR A LONG TIME I assumed it was because of my relatives, since my birthday meant a full complement of attentive grandparents, my two first cousins, my aunt and uncle, and my Saturday Night Club Aunt Junie and Uncle Gene, who wielded the movie camera. I was surrounded by blood relations and extended family, all of whom were quite willing to debate whether I had grown too much or too little. There was no hitting the mark in my family, which would be enough to drive anyone to tears.

My parents said it was because I was bad at sharing and that I got upset if another girl wanted to hold my new doll, but that wasn't it. I had a big-boned younger sister whose size eclipsed the almost three years between us, and she taught me pretty quickly how to share.

My crying remained a mystery to me until Sarah's fourth birthday, which involved setting a long table in the backyard, where she and a dozen friends each got to decorate a rag doll. I found the dolls at the art-supply store — blank muslin faces and bodies and three different colors of rag hair, so that every girl got one in the appropriate hue. We set out fabric pens, glue sticks, and trays of sequins, pompoms, ribbons, beads, and fabric scraps. The girls attacked the project with the focus of a transplant team.

When they were done and I brought out the cake, they turned that formidable energy on my daughter and sang "Happy Birthday" in a loud, collective warble. Sarah started to cry right away, and by the time they got to her name she had turned in her little wooden chair and buried her wet face against my arm. That was when I understood why we cried at our birthday parties. It had nothing to do with sorrow. No, we cried because everyone we cared about in the whole world was singing at us, and all that heartfelt affection was overwhelming.

ON LARRY'S FIRST BIRTHDAY — he knows this from the postmark — he got a postcard from his dad, a liquor salesman who was on the road more than he was home. It was the card that came with the hotel room, and the message was the classic big man, little man bit about taking care of mommy while I am away. A lonely boy and a smothered girl: How would Larry and I make Sarah's birthday right?

Our goal from the start was deceptively simple — to throw birthday parties that Sarah enjoyed. Larry wanted to convey his deep enthusiasm, so he pursued the niceties, from pretty postage stamps for the invitations to homemade ice cream from the little store across town. It did not matter that she was too young to appreciate the effort. True devotion did not require acknowledgment.

My challenge was not to hover, so I had to find a safe outlet for my formidable desire to celebrate. I decided to bake cakes, even though cake was the one dessert I had never been able to master. An early attempt at a family cake recipe, back in college, had come out the color and consistency of a hockey puck. I tried once more as an adult and had to crumble up the results and bury them under ice cream and syrup. I turned to pies instead.

But I wanted to bake birthday cakes. By the time Sarah and her friends were two, they had already made the Pavlovian connection between frosting and the passage of time. You could read it on their dewy faces: If we are getting two layers with sprinkles, if we are allowed frosting so sweet that we can feel the undissolved grains of sugar on our tongues, then someone is getting older, and it is time to sing.

That year, I bought a cake cookbook as big as a dictionary and preheated the oven a half hour too early. I watched the butter soften, I cradled the eggs in my hands to hasten their arrival at room temperature, and then I waited for the cup of milk to catch up. I placed my watch on the counter so that twenty seconds of beating would not become twenty-five. Like a man who wears a belt and suspenders because he trusts neither to do the job alone, I buttered and floured the pans and then lined them with wax paper, which I buttered and floured again.

And then, small culinary miracle, it worked. Year in and year out, the cake rose. I made my own butter-cream frosting and bought decorative piping tips and frosting bags. After a few years of successful two-layer rectangles, I acquired a cake pan shaped like a carousel horse.

There was no practical reason to do any of this, since there were a dozen bakeries and grocery stores within ten minutes of our house that would gladly have provided a cake decorated with little plastic horses or shaped like a horseshoe. No, I baked to be impractical, to drag out the celebration on purpose; I dug in my heels and made time slow down, if only for a day or two. Life stopped, except for the expectation of a fun party and the splitting and scraping of vanilla beans.

Sarah had days to get used to being the center of attention, and best of all, she had her little rituals of prebirthday delight. When I was done with the vanilla beans, she soaked the pods in a glass of milk, which she disliked the other 364 days of the year. She licked the cake-batter bowl and the spatula and watched me pipe frosting flowers on the cake. She waited to see if it would be candles or their little plastic holders that sent Larry to the market ten minutes before the guests arrived.

IT WAS OCTOBER 25, the night before Sarah's eleventh birthday, and she appeared at the bottom of the stairs when she ought to be asleep. Why wasn't she in her pajamas? She answered with an awkward shrug.

"Will you pretend I'm still a baby," she asked, "and get me ready for bed?"

She seemed a bit young to yearn for the good old days, but I knew what she meant. Need was so straightforward. She wanted to be carefree and dependent; she missed the utter irresponsibility that came of being incompetent, just like I missed standing between her and literal danger. We trudged upstairs, and I pulled one of Larry's old T-shirts over her head and held out her flannel pajama pants so that she could step in. I brushed her hair. I squirted toothpaste on the brush and she opened her mouth. Half her life ago, I sometimes brushed her teeth.

"Name them," she mumbled, from behind the toothpaste. I used to address her teeth by name, to buy the time to do a decent job: rhododendron, hyacinth, hibiscus, rose, daffodil. When I finished, she reminded me that she would still be ten when she woke up. She was born at 6:28 p.m., so she would not officially be eleven until tomorrow night. We agreed that it was nice to have a whole day to get used to the idea.

My mother was waiting for me when I got back downstairs, having arrived that morning from Scottsdale to celebrate this birthday in person. Norma is little. Arthritis and back surgery had nicked a half inch off her height, so she would never again be a statuesque five foot one-quarter inch, not even if she stood up straight, which was increasingly difficult for her to do.

She once owned a red spaghetti-strap sheath with a matching jacket, and she and my dad knew all the fancy cha-cha steps; now her spine threatened to take early retirement. She used to be a dish, though I hardly knew it at the time, but lately she was grateful for a pain-free hour at the driving range. She still had the trimmest ankles around. I wondered if old people got angry at the rest of us for treating them like another species, when every one of them was us once.

She held out a loosely wrapped packet that clearly had not come from a store, the tissue paper wrinkled and faded with age, no tape, no ribbon.

"This is for Sarah," she said, "but I wanted you to see it first." It must be important, and she must be afraid that Sarah would not think so.

Sarah already owned the closest thing we had to a family heirloom, my mother's gold locket from the Toby Circle, a family club started by her grandfather in honor of an older brother who never saw America. The club disbanded years ago, a casualty of geography and of smaller families who preferred to look ahead, so my sister and I were the last generation to get our own lockets. Sarah had to settle for a hand-me-down.

Now she would have another souvenir of the past: Inside the tissue was my Grandma Ethel's wedding handkerchief, transparent ivory and as fine as a butterfly wing. I was afraid it would turn to mist if I breathed on it. There was also a small note in Ethel's spidery scrawl, to document that she carried it when she married Harry in 1921. She dated everything — letters, recipes clipped from the newspaper, photographs, annual birthday cards — as though she knew that passing time would make a shambles of even the most vivid life.

When Sarah was six and Ethel was ninety-seven, they sang along with the birds in the nursing home lobby. When Sarah was eight and Ethel was nudging one hundred, I drove them and my mom out to our old house. We sat in the car in the alley and admired my maple tree, which had been a sapling when we moved in, while the girl who lived next door stared at us from behind her gate. Ethel had died six months after Sarah turned ten, just shy of 102. That was why my mother had come to visit, even if she hadn't thought about it.

"Maybe when Sarah gets married she can wear it," my mother said. "You know. Something old."

When Sarah was six, she asked me what a good age was to get married, and I said, "Thirty-four." I figured even if she rebelled and got married at twenty-eight, we were ahead of the game. Twenty-eight was as far away as Borneo, except that now we had the first item in her wedding wardrobe.

WE ALWAYS GAVE SARAH her presents on her birthday, even though this year her party was not for another two weeks, on a date when all her friends could attend. She got three T-shirts with horse slogans on them (her favorite showed the gaping jaws of a horse above the words THE LAST THING A CARROT SEES); a homemade certificate good for a pair of chaps, because we could not guess her size; and a sweatshirt that said HORSE LOVER on it.

When she got into bed, she said, "This is the best birthday I ever had."

I was pleased on a level more appropriate to news of world peace. There we were: a single day in which our notion of who she was coincided with her notion of who she was. To get the smallest detail right, when Sarah changed between the beginning of a sentence and the end, was a very satisfying thing.

The Martyr Imperative

PEOPLE BELITTLED OUR CONTENTED LITTLE FAMILY. THEY said:

Of course you're happy. You have only one.

Of course you're happy. You got a good one.

Of course you're happy. She isn't sixteen yet.

The more children a couple had, the harsher their judgment of us tended to be. Harry and his wife, Judith, who had no children, thought that we had our hands full only because there was something called a school night, when we could not join them for a last-minute dinner out. My sister, who raised two children alone, understandably considered us the farm team, ill equipped for the rigors of the Show. It took two of us, after all, to accomplish what half of her did.

At least she joked about it, which was better than the insults that I hoped were inadvertent. A put-upon mother of three once teased me by saying, "God only gives us what we can handle," a concept intended to comfort people who had too much trouble by implying that they were strong enough to thrive under difficult conditions. It was the spiritual upside of misfortune: You may be ill and out of bucks, living next to a chemical plant with a kid who steals from your wallet, but hey, God says that you're big enough to cope.

If it was the strong among us who could handle hardship, though, what did that say about people with easy lives? That they were weak, inept, short-sheeted on the coping skills? Anyone who charted the careers of certain pop singers knew that great things happened to bad people, but even the most cynical among us had to admit that the equation did not always hold. I might bc just as capable a human being as that sanctimonious mother of three.

Still, she got to me. "There's always work," I said, in feeble reply. "That ought to count for something, don't you think?"

Even some of my close friends carried a secret bias. Vicky had been the fifth front-row mom until she and her husband and two daughters decamped to Seattle. On one of their visits back, their daughter Jessi came over to play. The girls were up in Sarah's room, discussing which one of them would dress Sarah's new doll and which one would have to settle for a slightly older model, and as I walked by I heard Jessi say, "Well, you can have it, because my mom says you don't know how to share."

I winced, and watched as a wounded Sarah silently handed over the new doll.

The message was always the same: A family with one child was not a real family. University of Texas psychologist Toni Falbo, herself an only child, got tired of the idea in the early 1970s, when she was a graduate student at UCLA, and she went on to analyze more than five hundred studies to see if only children suffered "a disease in itself," as child psychologist G. Stanley Hall had written in the late nineteenth century. If so, it might be an illness worth catching: "Only children scored significantly better than other groups in achievement motivation and personal adjustment," Falbo told the *Washington Post.* They had slightly higher IQs, completed more years of school, and had significantly higher vocabulary scores on standardized tests. They had just as many friends as did other children, were picked for athletic teams as quickly, and scored lower on indexes of resentment.

They might even be better at sharing than kids with siblings were, because they were more confident that their turn would come. They grew up to make more money than children with siblings did and to spend less of it on psychotherapy.

The only quantifiable disadvantage they had was an increased risk of high blood pressure. And yet the most common reason parents gave for having a second child was to provide their first child with a sibling.

As more women worked, and waited longer to start their families, the landscape had started to shift: Single-child families were on the rise, up from 15 percent of households with children in 1989 to a predicted 25 percent in 2000. We were part of a growing trend, even if it did little to improve our standing among our peers.

I was prepared to yield on the issue of who worked harder — I accepted the idea that the woman with three children had much more to do than I did, just in terms of drive time and meal service. I had trouble with the notion that she was intrinsically a better person because she had reproduced more than once.

* * *

WE HAD ONE CHILD mainly because we waited too long to have any, and because three years later I miscarried, out of town, on April Fool's Day, somewhere between an appointment at a magazine, lunch with my book editor and my agent, and tea with a competing editor. We had not decided to have a second child, but we had not decided not to, and life holds surprises even for a couple who always uses birth control. I was starting to adjust to the idea of a new baby when my very brief pregnancy betrayed me, as I walked along Fifty-fourth Street, between Sixth and Seventh Avenues, in Manhattan; some hours later it was history.

I knew that the odds of a successful pregnancy and a healthy baby dipped after forty, and I knew my share of reasonably well-adjusted only children, including Larry. When I got home, we decided, formally, to stop at one.

I DID NOT KNOW what to make of the business about Sarah's being a "good one," since anyone who said that was quick to explain that her daughter was a good one, too, except perhaps for her irritating tendency to sleep late, to fail to do her household chores, to torment her little brother. Sarah might not have a sibling to harass, but did these parents honestly imagine that she was impeccable from dawn to dusk? That we never had a cross word? They were guilty of the doting-aunt fallacy — they extrapolated from public moments to a whole personality and forgot that Sarah was just as human as their kids were.

As for her not yet being sixteen, I am not an ostrich. I know that a driver's license alters the equation forever, as does a boyfriend. I know that there's no way to predict who she will be by then; if tween behavior were an absolute indicator of teenage personality, we would all be less apprehensive. But I resent the intrusion of the speculative future on my daily life. Whoever sixteen-year-old Sarah turns out to be, she isn't that person yet, so why let it cast a shadow over us now?

I would prefer to enjoy the enjoyable, for as long as it lasts. I do not carry an umbrella today because the weatherman has predicted rain by the end of the week.

Besides, I know girls who come home from college and occasionally want to spend time with their parents. Their mothers don't trumpet this happy state of affairs, like the sufferers do their suffering, but I've seen it just the same.

The problem is that we live in a yearning culture, fueled by celebrity and lottery billboards and various promises of eternal youth. The flip side of all that desire is the angst sweepstakes: Since most of us will never hit the jackpot, we compete instead for the more attainable title of saint, which requires only that we exaggerate every small dip in the day. Or perhaps we're embarrassed at how fortunate we really are, so we try too hard to prove that our lives are complex and full of meaning. Either way, we need someone else to have it better. Life is one big undergraduate Russian lit class, full of people who define happiness as being more miserable than the next guy.

I would like to take myself out of the running.

IN ANTICIPATION OF SARAH'S eleventh birthday party, we drove around town and took black-and-white photographs of the ten girls who were invited, had them printed on special paper, and hired a woman who ran a photo lab to teach them how to hand tint the portraits. They would not all go to the same school next year, and we thought this would be a nice memento of seven years together.

We set up a table in the living room. As soon as they sat down and saw the photographs, it started:

"I look terrible."

"I can't stand my hair."

"This is an awful picture."

"God, I look so stupid."

One or two, dumbfounded by the awfulness of being them, said nothing at all.

Here it was, the moment we had heard about since the doctor searched the ultrasound in vain for a penis. Boys went through an identity crisis as their voices changed and their chins sprouted stubble, but I could not speak to their distress because I didn't know one well enough to be privy to his pain. What I heard, from a mom or two, was that they were exceedingly good at placing blame for their discomfort anywhere but on themselves, which struck me as reasonable. Girls too often acted as though puberty were something they had done wrong.

I did not expect to get here so fast — I had hoped not to get here at all — but then, Sarah's generation had always been in a hurry. In October 1999 a group of pediatricians had revised the official age for the normal onset of female puberty from eleven to nine, to keep pace with their precocious patients. It only made sense that the accompanying emotional crises would come more quickly as well. I wished I had thought to rehearse a couple of responses before I actually needed them. Too late. I was the only woman in the room, aside from the teacher, who was a stranger to them. I did not know what to say, and yet I felt compelled to say something.

My mother's can-do generation took us at our miserable word and fought our perceived shortcomings with an arsenal of remedies that included an industrial-size aerosol can of Aqua Net hair spray, an eyelash curler, and a wand of turquoise eye shadow. My mother fixed parts of me that were not broken, which was why I wore a long-line panty girdle until my freshman college roommate pitched it into a snowdrift from our seventh-story dormitory window. The lesson of my youth was that the unimproved life was not worth living.

Not the best preparation for tonight. Despite my good intentions, I recited the same bland and useless reassurances that all enlightened parents now utter, because we would never imply that there is room for even constructive criticism where physical appearance is concerned:

"What do you mean, you look terrible?"

"That's a *beautiful* picture."

"Now, don't say things like that about yourself."

"I think you look great."

The girls responded appropriately: They ignored me. I could read the little thought bubbles floating above their heads, because I wrote the dialogue when I was them, all of it delivered with chilly condescension:

I hate my hair.

She doesn't understand.

Honestly.

MOTHERS.

I retreated to the kitchen, wondering how I could have managed to sound so dumb. I should have found something more lasting to compliment — kindness, a sense of humor — except that they would respond to that kind of flattery just the way my friends and I did when we were their age.

She's only saying that because she doesn't think I'm pretty.

This was brand-new: I did not need to torture myself over what to say, because nothing I said mattered. I dressed the salad and considered vinaigrette as a metaphor for life with girls: It worked well as long as you mixed it up; left to their own devices, the oil and vinegar would just as soon stand apart. Mothers had to work at being with their girls. If we didn't, we would stop speaking the same language, and then we would stop speaking at all. I was not ready to be relegated to the fringes of life, and I had a funny feeling that they were not quite ready for me and their moms to check out either.

The only option was to try again. Like my friend Carolyn said, Rewrite the script.

I made a second foray, and this time I fell back on my job skills and asked questions — which color would Julia pick for her shirt, how did Sarah mix the skin tone, who needed another Q-tip? No judgments, no firm opinions, just curiosity. They perked right up.

BY TEN O'CLOCK the living room was full of families eating cake and ice cream. A couple of years before, I had started to bake two cakes, one with frosting flowers and an inscription, and one backup plain cake so that there would be enough for the parents when they arrived to pick up their daughters. The front-row moms were in our kitchen often enough to know what was in which drawer, so Lori poked serving spoons into four quarts of ice cream, Jo Ann stacked the paper plates and napkins, and Phyllis dug around in the utensil drawer for forks, while I attended to cake and candles. Other unsuspecting parents showed up and succumbed to the promise of cake. Everyone gathered around to sing — and although Sarah's eyes shone, she did not cry.

Then we settled in to watch her open her gifts, several of which were no surprise to me; the front-row moms always called in advance to find out exactly what the birthday girl wanted. Julia gave her an alarm clock with a horse painted on its face and a packet of horse stationery. Lori and Roy's daughter, Emily, gave Sarah a squishy pillow shaped like a horse and filled with fragrant lavender, and Aviva, Jo Ann and Jay's girl, chose a soft red shawl.

I stood behind Larry's chair and took it all in: the squealing girls; Sarah's overheated joy; Phyllis's husband, Raphe, ducking into the kitchen for more cake; Jo Ann ignoring Jay's cholesterol count for just one night. Lori and Roy studied the photos lined up on the mantel, many of them from school trips and parties that Emily and Sarah had attended together.

When it was time to go, the girls got tangled up in good-night hugs at the door, congratulating each other on their beautiful portraits. Somehow they had come to love themselves again, and I thought, This ought to count as much as an outburst. We should never take happy for granted.

WHEN SARAH WAS EIGHT YEARS OLD and small enough to get pummeled on the playing field, she announced that she was tired of landing at the bottom of the heap in team sports. I said, Let's put her on a pony.

There was a small canyon on our side of town where people kept horses in stalls on their property and maintained a couple of riding rings, and teachers gave lessons there after school and on the weekends. It sounded just right for us, since the big commercial barns were too far away to be practical and too serious for a girl whose experience so far had been limited to wooden carousel horses and sleepy ponies tethered to a metal wheel. We found a teacher who was gaited just like the horses — two beats for the trot, three for the canter. She ran alongside, clinging to the horse's lead rope and shouting encouragement, as Sarah bounced in the saddle and laughed. Each of the horses we have since begged or borrowed or rented was the most beautiful horse in the world to Sarah, though each suffered from infirmities that ranged from overweight to chronic lameness.

When I was her age, I used to ride my bicycle around the neighborhood at top speed, imagining that I was flying toward the finish line on the back of the Godolphin Arabian, the subject of a book I checked out a dozen times before the school librarian insisted that I read something else. I purchased one horse figurine on every family vacation, from a plastic palomino to a tiny china foal, and the ones that survived the 1977 earthquake now stood on Sarah's dresser.

Several times I entered and lost the annual win-a-horse contest run by one of the Chicago daily newspapers. And I still have the gold pin with a pearl that I got for my sixteenth birthday instead of the long-forgotten horse my parents had promised me when I was eight.

Of course my parents did not get me a horse. I had a year of lessons, but after that I rode only with my dad on vacations. We lived in a suburb where neighbors frowned on dogs that lacked the self-control to make it to the median strip before they peed. Our entire house was a no-dirt zone. There was never a chance of a horse being part of the picture.

By sixteen I no longer even wanted a horse, but I complained anyhow. It was the perfect adolescent gripe — self-centered, unrealistic, about as appropriate as blaming my parents for my not being tall. Over time it became one of those jokes we tell on ourselves, a whole childhood condensed into one self-deprecating anecdote.

That was where it would have stayed if not for the convergence of three things that had nothing to do with me. I had read that teenage girls who were involved in a sport were less at risk for everything from eating disorders to depression; girls who got involved in athletics tended not to do dumb things to, or with, their bodies. I could see that Sarah had an affinity for animals, and vice versa — put six kids in a room with a puppy, and Sarah was the one whose face got licked. And we knew an older girl who rode a horse, a splendid kid who thought that a plastic bucket full of brushes and horse shampoo was the best present ever.

One girl was hardly a large sampling, but it was compelling. We lived in a city where girls got breast implants for their sweet sixteen, so someone who liked a bucketful of horse supplies got my attention. She might have been just as great if she had grown up playing chess instead, but chess did not satisfy the first two criteria for a new activity — the need for physical exertion and the compelling presence of a furry mammal.

One of the harshest things people can say about a mother is that she lives through her child — that she forces her daughter to do something the girl would rather not do, that she imposes her own unfinished business on a reluctant kid. Think of Mama Rose in the early days, before Gypsy decided that fan dancing could be fun. That was an oppressive relationship, no question — but what about a mom who wanted to revive a fond memory? Personal experience, however limited, had taught me that horseback riding could be fun and mountain climbing was way too scary, which was what distinguished me from, say, Vicky's husband, Hummie, who was terrified of horses but had a scar on his leg to prove his bravery in the great and vertical outdoors. I could introduce Sarah to enjoyable things but not enforce them, and then I would get out of the way if she picked something else.

I told a very skeptical Larry that we could try it and see what happened.

At first Sarah rode once a week, and then twice a week and more often in the summers. Before we knew it, she was riding whenever we let her. I took the occasional lesson so that Sarah would have someone to ride with if the opportunity presented itself. That was what I told people, and what I told myself; that was pretty much it.

Or so I thought. I had a birthday twelve days after Sarah's. Over a defrosted slab of her birthday cake, she and Larry presented me with my gift — a pair of riding pants. They had little fake-suede knee patches so I wouldn't slide off the saddle when I rode. I felt ridiculous in them, and they were exactly what I wanted.

8
The Great Outdoors

For a country steeped in the pioneer spirit, we do not get out much. A group called Visit Florida commissioned a survey about our "nature-based" habits and found that only 14 percent of us qualified as "heavy users" of Mother Nature's wares. The rest of us thought of the great outdoors as something to drive past. Another survey listed our most popular outdoor activities as walking and swimming, both respectable aerobic activities, and driving for pleasure and picnicking, which didn't quite qualify as getting back to the land. Theme park attendance was up, but that was manufactured wild, not the real thing.

Once the wagon trains had pushed west, we got very busy staying put. As a nation of immigrants, we seemed to prefer the comforts of the indoor life; our ancestors fled from somewhere and settled down, and defined in that context, success for subsequent generations meant the ability to avoid the elements. Wealthy celebrities and captains of industry colonized the less populous western states with sprawling second-home ranches because they could, and desperately poor kids got shipped to the country because otherwise they might never leave the block. The rest of us dropped by only occasionally or contented ourselves with wilderness shows on cable television.

I could live a full and happy life without ever thinking about hiking trails or poison oak, but Sarah had left with her sixth-grade class for a bus trip to Yosemite and a week of bonding, hiking, and adventure, so I thought of little else. I questioned the whole idea of these school trips — or rather, I questioned the imperative behind them, the straight-backed insistence that the children would go to Yosemite and love it. In previous years I had kept my mouth shut, and the children went to space camp, which Sarah kind of liked, and Catalina Island, which she definitely liked. I lectured myself sternly on the value of these expeditions, which exposed her to experiences we could not, or would not, provide.

Larry and I were cosseted suburban kids, each with a severely limited travel history. My mother always carried her own personal roll of toilet paper when we took our annual family car vacation so that we wouldn't have to use the gas station's inferior paper products. Larry's idea of roughing it is to eat take-out food straight from the containers. I slept under the stars once in my life, and for my pains I saw my dog nearly trampled by a cow. We were raised to depend on running water and indoor plumbing.

If we were not clear on why Sarah ought to sleep in a drafty cabin alongside large insects, it was our shortcoming, and we would not inflict it on our daughter.

The closer we had gotten to this year's departure, though, the more difficult it became. I had to stop talking to Phyllis because she disliked the idea of tween boot camp even more than I did. She couldn't think of a single good reason to send Julia, and she made me feel sane enough to consider speaking up.

I had my chance. In a nod to the concerns of urban parents, the school scheduled a parent planning meeting to walk us through the week's itinerary. The principal told us not to worry about the children's being out-of-doors from breakfast until dusk because there would be a sack lunch, something everyone liked, perhaps an apple and some peanut butter and jelly sandwiches. Sarah does not like peanut butter or jelly. Silently, I wondered if there were substitutions on the wilderness menu.

Then one of the teachers described the crowning event of the whole trip — the visit to the spider caves. The good news was that the caves got their name from a pattern the sun made on the front of the cave at a certain time of day, not from a resident herd of tarantulas. The rest of the news was not so good: The inside of the cave was so cramped and dark that the only way a child could get through it was to listen to the person ahead of her and go exactly where she was told to go.

I did not trust half the boys in Sarah's class in broad daylight, on the supervised play yard. What would happen if she ended up behind the kind of boy who gave the wrong directions on purpose, just to get a laugh?

Easy. She would move to another spot in line. She would not put herself in any danger. I don't know how I knew that, but I did.

I muttered loudly enough to be overheard that what we really needed was an Inward Bound program, a week of civilized family dinners where everyone sat up straight, tried a new vegetable, and participated in a conversation that had nothing to do with dirty socks or who forgot to take out the garbage. People chuckled and turned back to the packing checklist.

I took Sarah out for a big lunch on the Friday before the trip, determined to get several square meals into her before she left. On Saturday we reviewed the packing list, labeled everything but her tongue, and got ready for bed. We were so efficient that we had time left over to eat again. I cut three pieces of homemade pie, balanced them on top of glasses of milk, and carried them into our bedroom, where Sarah and Larry were reading.

"You guys are so well taken care of," I said.

Sarah took a plate and shot Larry a deadpan look. "Milk it for all it's worth," she said.

Ah, that Sarah. Droll, and pretty sensible about physical danger. No one would ever, ever say, Ah, that Sarah, never cracks a joke because she's too busy bungee jumping. Sarah, at eleven, was already dependably Sarah. She would not walk into a spider cave behind a goofus. I felt better. I was glad that I had not made up a nonexistent visit from a long-dead relative as an excuse to keep my kid at home. If she ended up hating the trip, at least it would be on her own terms. I could set aside my worst fears and settle for a week of mild emotional discomfort.

IF LARRY FUMBLED with the phone for two more seconds, I would have to kill him.

We had just finished a ridiculously expensive and fussy dinner, the sort of meal that made me wonder what I ever saw in multiple courses and waiters who folded the napkin the minute I stood up to go to the bathroom, only to hover until I returned so that they could drape it across my lap again. The last time anyone paid that much attention to my bodily functions, my mom was working with diapers. It was impossible to get through the meal without feeling that we had been had.

We were visiting the place where we lived before Sarah was born, back when we were a demographer's dream, a working couple with discretionary income and time on our hands. For tonight we were back in the cultural vanguard, where the question was always the same, whether we were dealing with arcane wild mushrooms, lethal stiletto heels, or thousand-dollar espresso machines with built-in burr grinders: Were we hip enough to embrace excess just because someone dubbed it the next new thing?

I was predisposed to love restaurants because I grew up in them. On a good Saturday morning, I went down to the Ira China Company with my dad; on a great Saturday, we drove around to call on his customers and I got to nurse a Shirley Temple while he sold stockpots and plates. But there is a fundamental difference between wonderful food and being taken to the cleaners, and we had wasted an evening being reminded of it. I should have known, the minute I read the menu's description of the exact location of the woods in which the wild game bird had met his maker.

What used to feel cool suddenly felt stupid. Next thing I knew, I would be extolling the virtues of an elastic waistband and a sensible haircut.

Perhaps this was all displaced angst, as we ended our second full day of Sarah's Yosemite trip. I had deceived myself with a surface cool for almost forty-eight hours, but the conceit fell away at the first burble from Larry's cell phone. Ten o'clock on a weeknight. This was not a business call.

Answer the phone.

He was moving at normal speed, but normal speed was for when we needed cash at the ATM machine. Finally, well after the third ring, he dug the phone out of his bag. He could have answered it, but he saw the look on my face and handed it directly to me.

"Hello?"

"Hi, Mommy."

There was a waver in her voice, but she was ahead of me, because I could not speak at all. I was awash in stress hormones; once I knew she was okay, I could admit how frightened I had been. Not scared of the wild, but scared in the way any parent is when the young child is far away and the phone rings late at night. Surprise is not a parent's favorite state of mind. The world screamed at us these days in a voice it never raised to my folks, who sent us outside after dinner and told us to play with the other kids until it got dark. It was a miracle of faith that we allowed our children to go anywhere at all, when one of the preschool safety lessons involved never talking to nice people who needed help searching for their lost puppies. There were accidents and predators, real threats and urban legends about kidnappers who stalked shopping malls.

A couple of years ago, I asked Larry how old Sarah would have to be before we let her walk the three blocks to the market, at dusk. He guessed ten. He guessed twelve. Then he got it.

"It's a trick question," he said. "The right answer is 'Never.'"

What if?

I tried so hard to keep that question at bay. I had to. Parents say that they worry because they love their children, and that is true, but somewhere inside of worry is a little worm of insult. Worry implies that our children are not capable of getting along, and Sarah could reasonably take offense if the first words out of my mouth were "What's wrong?" Anxiety is nothing more than devotion, soured, and I tried not to give in to it.

"I bet you're having a great time," I said, though it took effort.

She was until she tried to call us. On previous trips, the school had enforced a no-phone policy because it was easier for the kids to be cut off if they really were cut off. This year they had decided to allow after-dinner calls, and the peer pressure was tremendous. If the other girls in her cabin were calling home, Sarah would call home, too.

Her Luddite mother had told her to call our cell phone collect, not knowing that you cannot make a collect call to a cell phone. When that didn't work, Sarah called our house and got no answer. A vague desire to say hello congealed into a cold urgency. Luckily, a teacher with a phone card came to her aid.

And now, like me, she could relax. She recounted her communications nightmare with the giddy joy of someone who had just been reunited with a loved one, and I apologized for the mix-up, helpless, relieved, hoping that she would call every night from now on, hoping that she would not feel the need.

DAY THREE. We invited two couples over for dinner, people who knew so much about a lot of things that we were guaranteed an animated conversation about something other than children. But this was one of those odd nights when my subconscious commandeered the outside world. Everyone who walked in our front door wanted to talk about family.

My reproductive muse, Annette, sailed into the room with more than her usual verve and a story to tell. Both of her boys had intended to leave at dawn for the East Coast — the college freshman and the college grad, driving cross-country together with a couple of friends. The night before, near midnight, Annette had sold them on a new plan: They should leave immediately. They could get a head start on empty roads, drive all night, and be way ahead of schedule.

"And," she confessed to us with a big laugh, "they would be out of my hair eight hours sooner, though I didn't tell them that." She was ready for peace and quiet, she was ready to get back to her writing, and it was time for the boys she loved so deeply to get the hell out of there.

I could not believe it. Annette had never been one of those moms who let everyone know that she had far better things to do than drive to a swim meet or play rehearsal, nor did she rely on a squadron of hired helpers to raise her kids. She was lucky enough to have a choice, and she chose to raise her boys seamlessly. They were her life, the implication being that anything else would have been second-best.

If that was true, then who was this woman taking another helping of lamb?

It was Annette — not an empty vessel but a very funny woman who was in a hurry to do a ton of things. She was back with a flourish, and it did not feel like the manic rush of someone who would be on the depressive downslope tomorrow. It felt like the revival of a great old play. Opening tonight, *The Annette Story,* starring the actress who made the part famous twenty years ago.

I stared at her as though she were mad.

Laura, whose son was younger than Sarah, had only recently abandoned her efforts to add a sibling, so Annette's behavior must have seemed even stranger to her; she and her husband, David, were still preoccupied by infancy. The only explanation she could come up with was hormones: Women must be biologically hardwired to nurture kids when they need it and to turn them out when the time came.

Laura figured the split was inevitable. All the whining from parents about how the kids never called only meant that some people had failed to plan ahead for their free time. Separation was destiny. Someday she and I would be as blithe as Annette.

I wasn't sure how I felt about that idea. Wendy in *Peter Pan* was content with her adult life because she had forgotten how wonderful it was to fly. I didn't want to suffer endless longing when Sarah left, but I didn't want to forget either.

For the rest of the week, I meandered. I felt like a page of sheet music with the bar lines gone.

SARAH GOT OFF THE BUS on Friday afternoon the way she had gotten off all the previous school-trip buses, dirty, exhausted, craving a plate of Chinese noodles, wanting to kiss the dog. She was willing to accept my embrace as long as we kept moving toward the car.

She wasn't back an hour when Larry observed that she was markedly more self-possessed.

Already? He was right though; she was different. She had survived the raccoon skulking outside the cabin door and the middle-of-the-night stint as the designated bathroom companion. She had informed the trail guide that she had no desire to see the inside of the spider cave, and then she gathered her courage and walked through it anyhow. She found enough to eat.

She did fine. I was more pleased for her than I was mindful that she had gotten along without us, which struck me as progress on my part.

My life was closed to camping; our dream vacations all came with amenities. Sarah's life may end up that way, but it would be unfair of us to make the decision for her. I always puzzled over the question of what we wanted for Sarah, beyond the obvious hippie troika of peace, love, and understanding, because any list would by definition leave something out. It was too early in her life to leave something out, even camping.

I learned that from Larry. The first time Sarah jumped a little cross-rail jump on a pony, all of the color left his face. Truly, his complexion resembled the inside of a raw potato. This was the man who had asked the trainer, please, could one of the horse's feet be on the ground at all times. To him a good life was a life where horses did not jump — and yet there was Sarah, ever so slightly airborne.

He never said a word. He considered the size of the jump, which was less than twelve inches high, the proximity of the trainer, and the whopping smile on his child's face, and he sat there and waited for the blood to return to his brain. He taught himself to live outside his frame of reference, which struck me as one of the most generous things a parent could do. I tried to follow his example, to be glad, after all, that Sarah had gone to Yosemite.

WE FED THE EXTENDED FAMILY for Thanksgiving, and when it was over, I had a cold thought:

Sarah was better off without us.

I did not mean that literally. On a practical level, I was still a big help: I drove, tightened the girth, had credit cards, and was willing to lend her a scarf. I could do a French braid, and I knew to say *Vorrei fare una prenotazione* when we wanted to eat in Italy. I was a daily life resource — but in terms of her development as a person, I felt like less of a blessing.

I used to be the chat facilitator, a crucial aide for the only child of people whose best friends were childless. Too often in her early life, Sarah had been trapped by a well-meaning adult who wondered, loudly, "And what do *you* think, Sarah?" After a few such deer-in-the-headlight moments, I started stepping in to ease introductions, identify mutual interests, and then back away. I was helpful.

I thought I had struck a decent balance this Thanksgiving evening. There was no longer any need to help with our old friends, but one of them brought along a grown daughter who was interested in computers, so I mentioned a computer project of Sarah's, and they got to talking.

I mentioned a computer project of Sarah's. That, it seemed, was the felony. As soon as the last guest had left, Sarah complained that the grown daughter only spoke to her because I set it up — and by the way, a more sensitive parent would have noticed that her godfather, Harry, had ignored her rather completely. I had butt in, and not butt in, and I was wrong both times. Clearly, I had learned nothing at all from the incident with the teacher's aide who thought Sarah was small.

Sarah padded upstairs to get ready for bed. I scraped plates. Lyn Brown had said that there would be moments like these, when everything down to the alignment of the planets was mom's fault, when even the most reasonable adult was tempted to spit back in kind. She said, "Even when it's difficult, the onus is on the mother to be an adult." So I scrubbed the roasting pan, and I did not say any of the following things:

"You know what? Next year, we'll skip Thanksgiving. I don't need to do this."

"Honest to God, I have worked nonstop for two days, and for what?"

"Don't bother to say anything nice about the meal."

"I didn't see anybody else's mother offering to make Thanksgiving dinner."

Inside each one of us is a parody just waiting to be let out.

9 Bubble Grids

It was eight thirty on a dank Saturday morning in December, the sort of morning when any sane person would be in bed with coffee and the paper. The parents of a child with a terrible cold would have her in bed, as well, if the future were not tapping its foot and checking its watch.

We were in line in front of a card table at our assigned Independent School Entrance Exam location, to register Sarah and her head cold for three hours of bubble grids and an essay question. I hated this test, which promised to assign limitations just when a child might be vulnerable enough to believe them. For that matter, I hated all standardized tests, and I was not alone. As far as I could tell, the only ones who loved them were the people who made and sold the tests. Critics said that they failed to provide a realistic assessment of a child's abilities; that they discriminated on the basis of race, gender, or economics, or quite possibly all three; and that they made children crazy and their parents more so. Besides, we all knew a great person who always tanked on tests, so there.

And yet, we were one of only three families at our school that chose not to send our children to a test prep class or to hire a tutor. It was not arrogance. It was belligerence. A teacher once advised Sarah to think less about multiple-choice vocabulary questions — to pick the simple answer — because tests were not about nuance. I'm sure that was true. I'm also sure that it was way too soon to tell her what not to think.

A mom we knew peered into Sarah's snack bag and wondered, loudly, how we could send her off with only some cheese crackers and a bottle of water. The forgotten tangerine undoubtedly would have bumped her up a stanine in math, but it was too late for anything but regret. I started to explain that Sarah had a huge plate of pasta for breakfast, which was meant to fuel her through the morning, but then a new thought seethed to the front of my brain.

If this woman was so concerned, why didn't she offer to share something from her daughter's all-you-can-eat feed bag?

Because she was trying to pull the rug out from under Sarah. The fact that I hated myself for thinking such a thing in no way diminished its obvious truth. This was an ugly scene.

By the time we found the room to which Sarah's portion of the alphabet was consigned, I fully expected a healthier candidate to demand that she be ejected, lest her sniffles and sneezes distract the others and cost them a point or two. Larry handed me a tissue to hand to her, but she turned it down, twice. If I offered a third time, she could accuse me of not trusting her judgment, a bad place to be five minutes before a test that would determine her educational future.

She could use her sleeve.

As we backed toward the door with the other parents, I couldn't help but wonder: What if we rose up as one and hustled our children out of this room? What if we boycotted standardized tests? I was not brave enough to be a middle school Norma Rae, but I winced at the notion that one of these kids would feel sad because she got a three and her best friend got an eight, or because she heard her parents' worried whispers — the kind that stopped, abashed, as soon as she entered the room.

This was a test for us, too. It was so easy to love our children when they were toddlers and they rolled around the house like Slinkies in fat-suits, looking for new fun. A little kid was like someone who had been through a lot of therapy — they lived in the now, oblivious and resilient; ten minutes after a tantrum and a time-out, they were again the most cheerful beings on the planet. I sometimes felt worn out, when Sarah was small, and scared on her behalf of traffic and stairs and the broken drinking glass she mistook for ice and started to cram into her mouth, but that was different. Back then she needed us to survive.

Apprehension required the sorry adult ability to live in three time zones at once — now, later, and long ago — and it had surfaced more recently, as the world conspired to make us think more and more about the future. Tests were a formal prologue to adult life and a taunt to every parent: Go on, adore your child wholeheartedly now that we have on paper, in neat little columns with percentage signs, a sense of exactly what she can and cannot do.

Our job was to love the math flop as much as we did the math whiz, and to love the math whiz without idolizing her. We had to avoid endowing test results with too much meaning, even as admissions directors, consultants, and tutors did exactly that. Our school principal liked to quote experts who preached the gospel of personal best: We must ask our children only to work up to their potential, and then we must accept them for who they are.

Easier said than done. Tests implied victory and defeat, and they dismissed "average" as the place where boring children lived. We wanted our children to do well — and yet we wanted them to know that the results would not change the way we felt about them, not one whit, even if their best was somewhere in the statistical cellar.

When I got to the door, I whispered, "Sarah," and she turned around. I pointed to myself, crossed two fingers over my heart, and pointed at her.

I love you.

She did the same thing, and then she held up two fingers.

I love you, too.

GREAT KIDS FAILED to make the team, to get an A, to find someone to dance with at a party, to keep a friend. Someone else won the election for student body vice president, not because she was more qualified, but because she tossed candy into the audience after her speech. Someone else got the lead in the school play. A new dress did not fit its owner the same way it fit the model in the magazine, who herself was not a real person but a computer-modified image.

Consistency was child's play: mealtime, nap time, snack time. By the beginning of the end of elementary school, everything was up for grabs. Strangers issued verdicts, from test results to ideal-weight charts. There was no way to avoid or ignore them.

We could get plenty of help building winners, as though adolescence were one big Dale Carnegie success story, but please: The percentage of Nobel laureates in the general population was exquisitely small, and most of us did not grow up to star on Broadway or to invent a better replacement heart valve. I did not need a book to show me how to raise a star. I needed to know what to do when we went back to the test site in three hours to pick up Sarah.

I suspected that the way parents handled disappointment — how we defined it in the first place and what we did about it — was going to matter an awful lot. This was not a conclusion based on any scientific evidence, because the experts were very busy disagreeing with each other. Mary Pipher popularized the notion of sunken self-esteem that Gilligan and Brown first studied, sending parents scrambling for ways to make their daughters feel better about themselves. But a second wave of researchers suggested that the original work lacked academic rigor and headed off in the opposite direction. Revisionists warned that too much praise might backfire — instead of feeling better about herself, a girl could start to wonder why her parents worked so hard to make her feel worthwhile. If every other word out of their mouths was "wonderful," they must be trying to compensate for some pretty profound shortcomings.

Meanwhile, Judith Rich Harris wanted Larry and me to understand that hanging around with smart girls would matter more to Sarah's academic performance than anything we could possibly do. We had already put the genetic hex on her by serving up DNA that drew a blank on quantum physics but played a mean game of Scrabble. Beyond that, our behavior was largely beside the point.

So much for consensus. I could hardly blame the researchers, since it seemed to me that something as idiosyncratic as behavior — particularly family behavior, which involved overlapping idiosyncrasies — would by definition defy any attempt to draw lasting conclusions. The subjects were people, as were the researchers who studied them. I doubt I would trust anyone who claimed to have the one and only answer.

We were in a funny place. Sarah still took what we said as gospel, as she did when she was a little girl. The difference, now, was that she might decide to hate us for it.

Worse, she might not forget it. This was a terrible power. Our principal begged parents not to tell their children their test scores, since they couldn't boast or feel disappointed if they didn't know how they did. Larry and I agreed to tell Sarah that she had done fine, unless her bubble grids were misaligned and she scored a goose egg.

THREE HOURS OF COFFEE and vacant chat later, we were back to get her, helpless, huddled in the cold stone courtyard with everyone else's parents, waiting for the prison break. The kids came out bleary, either giddy with adrenaline or as wrecked as an old sponge. I overheard one mother who needed to know right this minute how quickly her daughter had finished each section, whether she skipped any answers, and why she picked a particular essay prompt. Another woman scooped her exhausted daughter into her arms with a kiss and an invitation to lunch.

Was the first woman overbearing? Was the second too blithe? Mother One would undoubtedly find Mother Two to be a bit too touchy-feely, since it was important to set standards and not let our girls off the hook. Mother Two would dismiss Mother One as a perfectionist, in danger of making her daughter feel like a failure no matter how well she did.

My instinct was that One would make her poor daughter nuts and that Two must have consulted her highlighted copy of the latest book on girls and self-esteem before she got out of her car, but who's to say? Daughter One might be a competitive type who thrived on having a demanding mother. Daughter Two might push herself so hard that she needed a break. If their mothers had gone just a step further, I could have dismissed them as bad moms and bad models, but they didn't. They sat just inside the edge of decency and good intention, which confused me.

Under the circumstances, theory eroded like an oceanside cliff after a downpour. When Sarah came out, she looked primarily like a girl with a head cold. The test was fine, she said. Now she wanted a nap and a bowl of soup. I could not tell if she was distressed or simply congested, but it seemed important to give her the benefit of the doubt. I wanted to know more. I did not ask.

We got her home and into bed, back to the reassuringly finite world of enough liquids and a fresh box of tissues. I had hoped that raising Sarah the adolescent would become clearer as we went along, but so far it felt like cleaning out the closet. There was always that awful moment at the start, when the chaos of disassembling the contents was far worse than the original mess, which at least had familiarity going for it. Suddenly there were clothes everywhere, cherished garments and fashion mistakes, and disorder ruled the day. The only way to survive the process was to endure it. Try something on, look like an idiot, toss it into the discard pile; try something else, feel right, fold and stack.

With diligence and patience, a new order emerged, but not for a while.

IN THE COMING DAYS — yes, there was an 800 number for parents who could not wait for the mailed results, and yes, we called it, too — several people offered an unsolicited tally of their children's impressive scores in the hope that we would reciprocate. One dad chanted a litany of eights and nines — oops, there's a seven, but it was the eights and nines he wanted to talk about — in the same eager way he tallied the perks of his upholstered life, as though having a bright child were right up there with owning a loaded BMW.

He implied that we must be holding back because we got bad news, in the hope that I would get angry and spill the details. For a cold moment I wanted to lie and say that Sarah had gotten all nines straight across the board. Would he love his son a stanine less?

I was more curt than I meant to be: "It is nobody's business except for the schools that look at the scores," I said, "and even then it's beside the point."

The only people I wanted to talk to were the front-row moms. By mutual agreement, we did not trade the actual numbers, but we did establish crisis parameters — no score above a five, say — and confirmed that each of our girls had survived. Four smart girls, four sets of smart-enough scores. Still, we confessed to small, reflexive mom worries. I dealt out three sets of reassurances and got three sets back, delivered with a mad and loyal sincerity.

Don't be silly, we told each other. Your daughter will be fine.

I WANTED VERY BADLY to believe that we would be fine. It was not part of my heritage. My parents eagerly took the world's empirical judgments to heart — not just grades but height and weight, the age of the family car, the amount of my father's annual bonus, my high school class rank, number of cavities, months in braces, consecutive weekends without dates. We were post–World War II suburban Jews, suspicious of anyone with a sunny disposition, always anticipating trouble, and numbers were reassuring. If I got an A, I must be smart. If I got a B, I had confirmed their worst fears. I grew up feeling that even my height — one inch shorter than the national norm — was somehow a failing on my part. A better person would be taller.

My test, on Sarah's test results day, was not to behave in the way that had made me feel bad a lifetime ago. If I resisted the urge to chase perfection, I could enjoy terrific for being just that, which sounded like a much happier approach.

When she got home from school, she asked, "How'd I do?"

I said, "Great," as offhandedly as possible.

"You going to tell me the numbers?"

"Nope."

"Okay."

Women Warriors

THE WEEKS BEFORE CHRISTMAS AND NEW YEAR'S WERE A manic scramble to get ahead. Several editors wanted an assortment of really small changes five minutes ago, on the last Monday before Sarah's winter vacation, and by eight o'clock that night, my brain resembled a tangle of deep-fried onion rings. All I wanted to do was crawl into bed and pretend to watch the TV news.

I was deep in blank despond when Sarah bopped into the room, ready for a good time. I stared at her from the recesses of my exhaustion and wondered if I was destined to disappoint her for as long as I put words on paper. The mom in me wanted gamely to spring into action and play a round of gin rummy or go fish, an endless card game that was all the rage. The writer wanted to lie absolutely still and flip between *Headline News* and MSNBC.

I imagined that every working mother felt like this sometimes, no matter what she did, but the illusion of being utterly alone enhanced the feeling of self-hatred. Nope. No working mother on the planet could be as bad a mom as I was at that moment.

"I bet you might like to have a mom who doesn't work," I said. Like Lori, who stopped working before her first child was born, or Annette, who went on hiatus for eighteen years, or that woman from preschool whose house always looked like a shelter-magazine layout.

"Why?" she said, not really paying attention. She has learned to edit out my more peripheral comments, which would serve me well in the long run.

"Well, because they have so much time."

What did I expect her to say?

Actually, Mom, I was *hoping for someone less distracted. I'd be much happier if all you had to think about was me.*

She wouldn't say that. I had set her up to say something nice. I was fishing for a compliment, willing to wait as long as it took to get a minnow on the hook. Shameless behavior, but I was incapable of better. I was too tired.

Sarah shot me a bewildered but admiring look.

"I bet you can go a whole twenty-four hours without running out of facts," she said. "Nobody else's mom can do that."

She kissed me and went to brush her teeth.

MORE THAN HALF of all mothers who have children under the age of eighteen work for compensation. I attach that qualifier reflexively, so that women who are full-time wives and mothers, for no pay, will not take umbrage. Jobs are not a line item on the martyrdom spreadsheet but a cold economic fact, and most gainfully employed moms do not look like the glamorous working moms we see in magazines, with a baby on a designer hip and an entourage lurking offstage.

I used to think that all women my age worked, because the ones I knew did, but I found out I was wrong the minute Sarah started preschool. The world was lousy with full-time mothers, some of whom had worked, briefly, before they got pregnant, some of whom had stopped working the minute they got engaged. I had no idea they existed. Worse yet, they were satisfied with their lives. They did not need to be me.

In my defensiveness, I wondered: Had they napped through the women's movement? Did they not comprehend that they were sailing toward the same existential ennui that made Betty Friedan set pen to paper in the first place?

I did not ask, because I was too busy feeling superior. I might have raggedy cuticles and no time for skin care, but I was all those things a new woman was supposed to be. Competent, relevant, accomplished. I lived in the larger world.

As it turned out, that was exactly why they felt superior to me.

They said, "I don't know how you manage. Little Joy takes up every waking moment."

And I heard, You can't possibly be doing a decent job of being a mom, with all the time you spend working.

"I'm just so grateful to Fred for making it possible for me to stay home with Gina."

Your husband must not make very much money.

"I think it's great you travel for work sometimes. I've never spent the night away from Billy. I just don't have it in me."

You, of course, have ink in your veins and a computer keyboard for a heart.

"Oh, do you have to leave already? Well, Sarah can sit with us."

Poor child. Such abandonment issues.

Okay, I was projecting. The problem is that I love to work. Growing up, the three panels of our family triptych read: Get a job, own your own home, and always live near a teaching hospital. I might not love the economic imperative of having to work, but the work itself has mattered since the day my eighth-grade English teacher made me promise to write for the high school newspaper. I earn a living, which ought to be worth something, as far as role models go, in an economy where most of us will have to do just that.

In the early days of my career as a politically correct mom, I could condescend with the best of the hard-liners: Stay-at-home moms were out-of-date, out of step, destined to be left behind by their ambitious daughters — or not, if they raised another generation of men who headed into the world and women who did not. Women who stayed home to raise women who stayed home — it made me think of my childhood reading textbook, which featured a picture of a girl and a boy holding a book whose cover featured a girl and a boy holding a book whose cover featured a girl and a boy holding a book, on to infinity.

I clung to a tidbit of information I got from the working mother of an older girl: In her informal sampling, daughters of working moms had an easier adolescence than did daughters of full-time moms, because working moms practiced what they preached. "If your mom tells you that you can go out in the world and do something great, and she's out there herself doing something interesting, then it makes sense," said the mom. "And you've experienced the larger world, so you believe you're capable of being a part of it. But if your mom says, You can do anything, and she's at home taking care of the kids, it doesn't quite compute. A girl has to reject her mom to do what her mom wants her to do. It's just harder to make sense of things." The one thing working mothers did not have to contend with, it seemed, was cognitive dissonance.

Then there was Lori, who at twenty-eight had informed her boss that she had not completed her corporate strategy form for the coming year because her only strategy was to start a family — Lori, who went into labor with her first daughter on the way home from a marketing meeting and never went back. She was a full-time mom who ran her household with an efficiency that reflected her corporate background, and in spite of ourselves, we got to be friends. She would not live my life on a dare, nor I hers, but we could not sustain the kind of disdain that fueled so much of the working-mom controversy.

The lines began to blur, and I came to see moms as busy or not busy, the issue of income aside. I grew impatient with women on both sides who were as doctrinaire as I had been: working mothers who groused about the overrated purgatory of rearing children, and stay-at-home moms whose cars sported those sanctimonious bumper stickers that read, "All mothers are working mothers."

The reciprocal insults were so awful. Full-time moms had been known to run a calculator tape on what career moms spent supporting their work habit, to prove that we could afford not to work if we just stopped paying for nannies and baby-sitters and after-school programs and private day care. Our dirty little secret was that many of us worked because we wanted to, which sounded, when the opposition said it, like an unspeakable sexual perversion — something that a healthy, decent American woman would never consider doing. Working moms could be just as nasty, dismissive of full-time moms as though they were a third sex, breeder stock, incapable of anything more taxing than driving the family van and choosing the right fabric softener.

The hard line was always simpler to follow than the more complicated truth, but seven years of Lori had forced me to acknowledge that working moms were not necessarily more highly evolved. It was possible to have a friend on the other side. In the calm paranoia of a sleepless night, unencumbered by reason, I had a new thought: What if the hostility between working moms and full-time moms were a conspiracy perpetrated by the guys, who stood to profit from the enervating effects of all that scrapping? The best way to stay on top, after all, was to make sure that the insurgents were too busy fighting each other to mount a combined offensive. Presidential candidates have won elections, and dictators entire countries, thanks to infighting on the other side.

AT THE NEXT parent association meeting, a mom asked plaintively why her daughter always wanted to talk to her at bedtime. What could she do to shift the important conversations to a time of day when she felt more alert?

The principal answered, "Because your daughter feels most relaxed and at ease right before she goes to sleep," to the first question, and, "Absolutely nothing," to the second.

Finally, a tidbit of advice that sounded right to me. A good mother listened when she was so tired that the muscles in her eyelids burned from the effort of holding them open. She listened until her daughter poked her and said, "You're asleep," at which point she lied and swore she wasn't. She listened while a book went unread, or an adult conversation was delayed, because she felt like an idiot the one time she had opted for a TV cop show instead.

I did that on a night when I was too tired to sleep, too tired to make sense of whatever it was that Sarah wanted to tell me. Since I do not drink to excess, my only hope of winding down was a mind-numbing police procedural. I kissed Sarah good night and told her I had to collapse, and halfway down the hall I regretted it. Whatever she was going to say to me that night was gone, irrevocably gone, and I was a dunce for not having hung on ten minutes longer.

Of course, at the time, ten minutes was an eternity, but I wish I had stayed. The illogic was inescapable and seductive: If I listened now, she would talk to me when she was older.

ON THE LAST DAY OF SCHOOL before winter vacation, I constructed a shrine to having it all: Work all morning, hand out holiday gifts at school, grab Sarah when the kids got out at noon and take her to a horseback lesson, drop her in West Hollywood to crew for a friend's play, and get back home in time to check into a beachfront hotel with Larry for a romantic one-night celebration of our sixteenth wedding anniversary. I arranged for the baby-sitter to pick up Sarah after the play. Larry arranged for a room with an ocean view and a VCR, which meant that we might get to watch a movie of recent vintage without a single interruption.

It would have worked, if not for the retail imperative on the second-to-last Friday before Christmas in a city where nothing is nearby. The traffic was so slow that I could check price tags in the store windows from the driver's seat. At 3:20 I called Larry from outside the theater where I had delivered Sarah an hour late. I would never get home before five.

"The hotel just called," he said, with a resigned sigh. "They wondered where we were." The childless manager had kindly offered him a rain check, as though other weekends would be less busy, and the baby-sitter showed up anyway, so we had time for a nice walk to the video rental store.

Gift-Giving

A SCHOOL VACATION IS LIKE A HONEYMOON: HAVING MADE the commitment, you get to leave distraction behind and find out to whom you have promised your life.

When school was in session, free time with Sarah was at a premium. Between school and riding and homework and friends — and this year, the filing of applications to new schools — there were days when we had less than four hours with her. She could brush and floss her teeth or get into bed on time or talk to us, but not all three. She would barely be broken in before we sent her off to college.

For the first time, I decided to take off the week between Christmas and New Year's, and I encouraged Larry to do the same. People who had office jobs respected the holiday season — they came in late and left early, took long lunches, spent the afternoon shopping. Life was one big voice mail in-box, and I was ready to ignore work with the best of them.

Enough. Sarah was home, which was like ice cream in the freezer: I want it, whether it spoils my dinner or not.

ON THE FIRST SUNDAY of winter break, Sarah was down on the tennis court wielding a racquet whose head was as big as her torso, while Pat, the instructor, counted how many times they could hit the ball back and forth. I had not seen her play for months, so I was astounded that they had anything to count at all. When they got to ten he wanted twenty, and when they got to twenty he asked for thirty. Pat never lost his patience, never gave up, and always behaved as though the next try would be better. He knew how to expect a lot without sounding like a tyrant, and he knew when to back off. He believed in Sarah.

Pat would make a good mother.

People who barely knew Sarah thought of her as the quiet, big-eyed kid who always has her nose in a book, which was true but not complete. If she liked the crowd, things loosened up considerably.

With Pat she kibitzed nonstop.

"I can't. I have to have some water."

"Thirty? You said twenty."

"That was in that was in that was in."

When she got off a clean shot, she glanced over to where Larry and I were sitting, to see what he thought. He smiled and nodded his approval, and he got back the kind of smile that would make anyone decide to have a family. It was not a conscious, considered smile, the kind that came in response to a compliment or a good report card. It had less to do with the tennis ball than with having a father who paid attention.

We think that it is our job to impart the lessons of life to our children, that information flows only one way, from the authoritative parent to the growing child. Not when I see that smile. Sarah knows something I used to know, and I want it back: that it is possible, in the midst of everything, to be absolutely happy.

MY DAD AND I shared a series of vacation trail rides on barn-sour horses, which I remembered as clearly as if they were movies, down to the pinto I rode in Colorado and my dad's ability to chain-smoke without dropping the reins. We did not have to work very hard — no matter what we did, the horses slogged out and cantered home — and we did not talk about much beyond the beautiful scenery, but I loved those rides, and I loved my dad for going with me when I knew he would rather be sunbathing.

It turned out that I was as typical as toast: JoAnn Deak, a school psychologist on the stump for adolescent girls, spoke in Los Angeles last year, and what stuck with me was a comment she made about a dad's attention mattering more to a daughter than even the most supportive mom's. When I talked with her later, she admitted that she had no hard data to back up her assertion and that she might have exaggerated the bit about dads having a value edge over moms. She did so to make a point. Deak has spent more than twenty years working with the families of teenage girls, and she thinks that dads ought not to settle for being breadwinners. She had a sense, born of her experience, that their encouragement and approval meant a lot.

I came home after that speech and asked Larry to pick something he and Sarah could do together — and please, to leave me out of it.

He chose tennis, since he was once good enough to teach it and would be able to practice with Sarah between lessons. When he found Pat, Sarah gallantly insisted that Larry take a lesson as well. Every Sunday they headed off, Larry with the crossword puzzle to work during Sarah's lesson, and Sarah with the comics and a book to read while Larry played. Simple as that, Sunday mornings belonged to the two of them.

They always invited me to come along and bring the dog, but I did not say yes as often as I might have. It was a small, self-imposed discipline. I could always use the time to catch up on work or to sit still, but what I did was frankly beside the point. I had the glimmer of an idea: If I sent Sarah off without me as part of the normal scheme of things, she might not feel the need to stage a palace coup to assert her individuality. This was not a stunning notion — the summer-camp industry was designed to build a child's independence — but we didn't raise a camper, so we had to figure out other ways not to suffocate her.

WHEN JOHN WAS still alive, Carolyn would sometimes drop him off at the library, or at a bookstore, while she and I grabbed a quick lunch. In the wake of his death, we abandoned the little café where we used to meet, having decided that we needed more joy than a damp chopped salad, hold the onion, could provide. We moved to a fancy place by the beach, where we could stay close to fiscal responsibility as long as we ordered only one course.

We had a date right before Christmas, and since there was no school, Carolyn asked me to bring Sarah along. When we sat down, she handed Sarah a tiny wrapped box. Inside was Carolyn's teenage charm bracelet, thick with silver charms from a family friend who had traveled the world and sent back souvenirs. Sarah examined each one with her fingers, exclaiming over a tiny silver hen that lifted off its nest to expose three tinier silver eggs, a pelican with a fish in its mouth, a mailbox that opened. Charm by charm, city by city, Carolyn introduced us to a stranger who had seen the world, loved Carolyn, and never knew that someday a girl named Sarah would take her treasures home.

That was one thing a child could do: She carried lives with her, stretched them further into the future than they otherwise would have gone. A lifetime from now, she might decide to bestow this bracelet, and its stories, on some other little girl whom Carolyn and I would never meet.

From there Carolyn and Sarah progressed to a detailed discussion of Dick Francis mystery novels, and since I was the only one at the table who didn't read mysteries, I got to listen, the way Sarah had, all those years when she was too young to take part. I had nothing to contribute to the conversation, and I felt a little miffed at being left out, but I tried to concentrate on all the interesting things they had to say to each other.

My left rear tire went flat while we were at lunch, so Larry drove over to rescue Carolyn and Sarah. I waited in a misty rain for the Auto Club and then hobbled to the tire store on one of those donut spares that never look up to the job. I spent the remainder of the afternoon in the tire-shop waiting room, riffling through old magazines, feeling displaced. Moms get shed slowly, inevitably, kind of like snake skin. Today was relatively easy, I guess, since Sarah was perfectly happy to have me around as long as I didn't interrupt the bracelet story or the mystery roundtable, as long as I did not monopolize Carolyn or treat Sarah like anything less than an equal guest at the table.

These were the early days of independence. I could look down the road and see, for the first time, where a mother's side of the hostilities could start. When I sent Sarah off to tennis without me, I was the virtuous architect of her independence, but when she enjoyed lunch without any help from me, I was superfluous. A mom might have trouble making the transition from leading lady to a bit part.

The odd thing, according to Lyn Brown, is that some amount of conflict is a good sign; the trick is for a mom not to take it personally. "Mothers complain that girls are difficult," she said, "but that is the most important part of the connection. They're forging their own identity in relation to the person who's most intimate with them. It's a sign of maturity; they need a safe person they can go after. It's an incredible compliment to a mother, even though it feels terrible."

A girl needs to push off from the side of the pool, that's all it is, but a mom can get irritable and respond in kind, which is a very bad idea. She can take evolution personally. She can make the fundamental error of wanting attention when it is not her turn.

Today was not my turn.

A FEW NIGHTS LATER, we went to a friend's for Christmas Eve dinner, an annual event since the days when the kids were too young to know if they liked each other. Now they were in tween purgatory — old enough to know that they might not socialize with each other, given a choice, but too young to drive and too young to spend a long night home alone. Two girls in fancy clothes and two boys in dress shirts, held hostage by their parents' holiday agenda.

We were putting on our coats to go home when it clicked, just like that, over a new CD of Beatles hits. The hosts' son had just bought it, and Sarah, who had seen *A Hard Day's Night* the day before, intended to as soon as she could get to a music store. The boy launched into a defense of his favorite cuts, and every time he stopped for breath, Sarah jumped in to talk about her favorite scenes from the movie. The other two kids listened, rapt, and provided an assortment of appropriate noises — an insider's chuckle, an envious sigh or two. Oh, to be eleven and know what to say.

I nudged Larry and held a finger to my lips.

Look at her.

One by one, the other parents noticed. Silently we watched the quartet in the corner: the sports fan, the brain, the popular girl, and serious Sarah, cut off from those of us who had met the Beatles on an earlier pass.

An adult breathed too loudly and it was over, to sheepish laughter on all sides. Sarah came over and dropped her head against my shoulder. She would be asleep in the backseat of the car before we got to the freeway, though the days when I could lift her out, carry her upstairs, and get her into her pajamas, all without waking her, were over.

I NEVER SAW a house like this when I was a kid: red velvet upholstered furniture, a fake leopard-skin rug, a painting of Las Vegas chorines across the room from a Simpsons pinball machine, an ottoman stacked with art books, and everywhere, the remnants of an extravagant Christmas. My childhood experience ran to a paneled recreation room, plastic slipcovers, and a pastel powder room for the guests, and Larry's parents' Philadelphia apartment was so tidy it squeaked. I liked to think that Harry and Judith's house would shake up any inherited notions Sarah might have about what, exactly, constituted home sweet home.

We spent New Year's Eve with our invented family — Harry and his widowed mother, Dora, who had come to Los Angeles from Poland by way of Cuba; Judith and her widowed father, Handel, an opera singer who lived in London; her sister and her brother-in-law, who visited once a year from Ireland; and the three of us. We ate an Italian/Cajun feast big enough for twice as many people, and then we settled in to watch televised midnights in earlier time zones while we waited for ours to arrive.

We would never be family, not in the usual sense, for our shared memories go back at most no further than college. Still, there is something to be said for unrelated relatives. We get a whole new audience for our childhood stories and never a challenge from an aunt who was there and swore it didn't happen that way. We listen by choice, not biological imperative, and besides: If shared childhood memories were so essential to meaningful relationships, arranged marriages would be a lot more popular. Bonding is bonding, whenever it happens.

Just before midnight, Handel glanced over at Sarah, the lone child, swaddled in a red velvet blanket on a big cushy chair, her head resting on a red velvet pillow. There was something mystical about her, as she stood at the departing edge of her own childhood. The same girl who argued with Harry about girls' schools could still pull a pout or demand a cuddle, and the instability — a young woman? a little girl? — made the rest of us shift between now and then, between life and memory. We all did it: Carolyn with her charm bracelet, Harry with scenes from his bootstrap childhood, Judith with cautionary tales of a headstrong youth. Sarah stood at the doorway to the past, and sometimes we liked to visit there.

Handel told her that when he was her age, the adults always sang the children to sleep on New Year's Eve. Given Handel's profession, it was hardly an idle reminiscence. I waited to see if he would sing. I would not intrude and ask him to, for this was a story he was telling Sarah, not me, and I had gotten in trouble with her before when I intervened. He smiled at her, and it was all she could do to smile back. Conversation had deserted her an hour ago, and she was so tired that her eyes had turned to glass. Her fingers played idly with the blanket fringe, to keep her awake.

She could not bring herself to ask him either, but she made great show of wrapping herself up in the blanket and moving from the chair to the couch, where she stretched out, announced loudly that she was going to sleep, and closed her eyes.

Then she opened them, to see if a song was forthcoming.

It was not. The video celebration in Las Vegas distracted us, and Handel turned to the television to watch the fireworks, spared from what might have been too much memory. There was no song, only exclamations at the tackiness of this costume or that. The moment was gone. I was full of regret for not having asked.

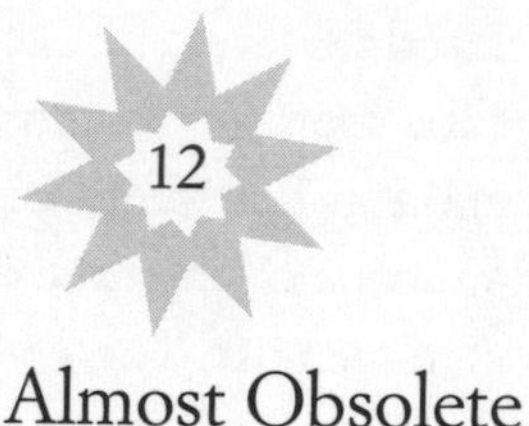

Almost Obsolete

GOING BACK TO SCHOOL IN JANUARY WAS HARD AFTER weeks of holiday socializing, so Sarah and Julia lobbied for frequent homework dates, usually at our house, since there was no little sister to intrude. Toward the end of the month they asked to go to Julia's one afternoon, with a crazy logic that only two-job couples could appreciate: Julia's child-care person came on Tuesdays, because both her parents got home late, but her younger sister had after-school plans. If Julia didn't come home, the child-care person would have nothing to do.

Trust was on the table, since the girls' usually impeccable study habits at our house might be a function of having a couple of enforcers around.

"Okay," I said, "as long as you do the homework."

"If we have to," said Julia, a night owl who could stay up late and still put her socks on straight in the morning.

"You have to," I said, the parent of a morning person. "Those are the terms of the deal." I told Sarah to be home at five.

She forgot. At 5:15 I walked up the street to get her, but she begged to stay longer. All she had left was a couple of math problems, and they had not yet gotten to the fun part of the date. She got an extension to 5:45.

By six o'clock the excitement of having a newly independent daughter was gone. Sarah was late a second time, evidence of a general disregard that was clearly our fault. We were too laissez-faire about the building blocks of adulthood, and not just punctuality. We were bad role models on any number of levels. We could be neater; we could try harder not to misplace the checkbook. If we had ever sorted the mail on the day it arrived, she would have been home by now. We berated ourselves to the tick of the clock. Sarah had lost a riding helmet and two sweatshirts in the last twelve months, and we had not exacted any punishment. Why on earth would she bother to come home on time?

The minute she walked in the door, we did what any parent who had fallen short would do — we overreacted. We told her there would be no study dates for a week — and by the way, where was the helmet, those sweatshirts, the sweater with the horse's head knit into it, and anything else that might be missing?

She got defensive, a completely appropriate response when the two adults she loved most in the world started berating her.

"What was I supposed to do?" she asked. "Keep running into the kitchen to look at the clock?"

In a spin worthy of Gene Kelly, she had turned her being late into our expecting the impossible. How could she simultaneously finish her homework and be in the kitchen checking the time?

"That's not an answer," I said.

"But it's the truth," she replied. "What do you want me to do — *lie to you?*"

SPEAKING OF FABRICATION, we learned after dinner that Sarah had a bit more than a few math problems to finish — in truth, she had half the math assignment, a freehand drawing of the United States, and a Web search for photos of Japanese emperor and empress dolls, for reasons she did not have the time to explain.

We had been hoodwinked. Larry launched into a tortured analogy about how the insurance company would raise his rates if he scratched the fender of his car, which I assumed he intended as a moral lesson about the consequences of irresponsibility. I wished that Sarah had not interrupted him, if only to find out exactly where he was headed.

"I'm too young to drive," she said, with weary condescension.

"Look, we need to have some kind of mutual understanding, now," I said. "Because when you're sixteen and out with your friends, and you say you'll be home at midnight and you don't come home and we don't hear from you, we'll be tearing our hair out. And then the next time you won't get to go."

"I'm not sixteen," she said. Then she laughed, out of nowhere, and headed back to her desk.

ONE NICE THING about a horse is the need to pay attention right now: Were his feet clean, was the girth tight enough to keep the saddle from sliding off, was Sarah's helmet on straight, and was that truck rumbling down the street going to scare him? There was very little future, on a horse, except for the distance between here and there.

I was focused on daily life, horsewise, so I did not see the milestone coming: Sarah's trainer, who specialized in beginners, decided that Sarah should move up to Meredith's class, the legendary Meredith, reputed to have been one of the loveliest riders ever seen before a bad hip took her out of circulation, trainer to generations of riders and a handful of other trainers. Meredith taught girls who owned their own horses and jumped big jumps. Sarah and I were justifiably intimidated. She went into the ring on a borrowed gray pony for Meredith's beginner's class, and I took a seat in the weathered wooden bleachers to watch the master at work.

Meredith sat at the end of the bleachers with her bullhorn and her propane heater, and she gave Sarah the slow once-over.

"Take your feet out of your stirrups."

Without a word, Sarah hung her legs straight down. Meredith studied the relation of stirrup to anklebone and pronounced the stirrups too long — at which point Sarah looked over to me for help. Reflexively, I got to my feet.

"You can shorten them yourself," Meredith said. She shot me such a withering look that I sat right back down.

"If you don't let them struggle," she said, "they never learn it for themselves."

Just like that, sidelined, relegated to the endless bleachers all over the country where useless but supportive parents watched their children. We might sneer at the couch potato, but they had comfier chairs and better refreshments than horse parents, and they did not get a noseful of dust every time their beloved child shot past. It felt awkward to be a spectator: Where was dignity without purpose?

Fixing a stirrup is not easy, at least not the first five or ten times. It hangs from an adjustable leather strap that fits into a metal clasp tucked high under the saddle flap. Sarah had to tug at the strap until she could get at the buckle, and then unbuckle and rebuckle it, without falling off the pony. Worse, she had to do it in front of an audience of impatient girls who already knew how long their stirrups were supposed to be.

I watched her struggle to keep her balance while she yanked on the strap. I watched the pony, who was, after all, a living being who might not enjoy all the squirming. I sat on my hands, even when I saw a glint of tears, and finally, after much pulling and sighing, Sarah managed to undo the buckles and shorten both straps. The lesson could begin.

I was ridiculously proud. Look at that girl and her stirrups, I thought to myself. Look at that mom, who knew better than to meddle, almost.

CAROLYN'S TWO DAUGHTERS inherited their mother's belief that a party is an antidote to almost anything life serves up, so they invited a handful of us to tea at the Beverly Wilshire Hotel, on the theory that enough scones and cream would blot out the sorrow of Carolyn's first birthday without John. Two of us arrived early, so we waited for the other guests in a little anteroom. Linda was eager for company: Her grown son had just gone back to New York, where he has lived for seven years, and his visit had unsettled her, as his visits always did.

"I prefer it when he's in New York," she said, "because I get into a rhythm of life without him." Every time he came back, she remembered how much she missed him.

"You never get over their leaving," she said, without a trace of self-pity. Linda is a psychologist, so everything she said carried a considered weight. If she said we didn't recover, I imagined that on some level we didn't.

"That's what I'm starting to think," I said. "And anyone who says you get over it is lying." I didn't actually think that, not yet, but I wanted to know if she did.

"They are lying," she said.

"Or lying to themselves."

"That, too," she said.

We were like any other kind of addict, except that our drug of choice was love. A twelve-step program was probably inevitable, since they already existed not just for alcohol and drugs but for shopping and eating. If someone with a Milky Way jones could find a support group, empty nesters could not be far behind.

Hi. I'm Diane. I've been a mother for twenty-four years, and it's been six months since I last saw my daughter.

Hi, Diane, the group would respond, with enthusiastic applause.

I did not look forward to a lifetime of missing my child, nor an afternoon talking about it. When the other guests arrived, I maneuvered my way to a seat between Carolyn, who managed to keep her grown daughters close, and a woman I had never met. Dana had a son in college and a laugh like a waterfall. I hoped for lighter conversation.

Dana's son had recently told her, in great and humorous detail, of a friend's experience with a controlled substance.

"Did you ask him if *he'd* tried it?" I asked.

"Well, no," she replied. "I figured he was talking to me, and that was the most important thing. It won't kill him if he tries it." Even if her son had consulted her in advance, she said, she would not have expressed her disapproval, since what mattered most was that he told her anything at all.

That was a cold choice — down the line, I could be protective or informed, but probably not both. Under what circumstances would I get to say, I am horrified, stop it right this minute? Years ago, as soon as Sarah was old enough to comprehend, I gently extracted a promise from her that she would never, ever smoke; one relative was too many to lose to the demon weed. How naive of me to rely on a promise made out of a child's love, not informed reason. How foolish to imagine that she would consult me if she changed her mind once she was grown.

Right now, Sarah aspired to jump two-foot fences. "Two feet is high enough for me," she said staunchly, as the older girls jumped three feet and higher. Two feet was high enough for her parents, too, but as I listened to Dana I realized that our preferences were beside the point. Two-foot fences were just the start. There was an array of more provocative teen choices Larry and I would have opinions about, opinions that would not necessarily coincide with Sarah's. We had to figure out how to state our position without being so absolute that Sarah stopped talking to us.

There were two obvious ways to slip. Pal parents said yes all the time because they were not ready to be old. Clingy parents said no all the time because they were not ready for their children to be old. Either way, parents were too busy fleeing their own mortality to listen, and at some point a child simply stopped asking — why bother, if the answer was always the same? Those parents were exiled to Siberia, where no one ever told them anything. I did not want to go there.

Dana was probably right. The most we could hope for was to stay in the loop.

LIKE IT OR NOT, being a teen means taking chances. Brain researchers have taken ever-more-sophisticated scans of brains at work, and one of their findings would chill the heart of anyone whose child just asked for the car keys. The limbic system, the part of the brain that feels adventurous, matures before the prefrontal cortex, the part of the brain that exercises good judgment. As a species, we go through a phase when we want to do things that are not good for us, except that we don't know they are bad until later in life.

The activity center of the adolescent brain is raring to go. The judgment room has a big "vacancy" sign hanging over the door. Bad intentions do not make your son or daughter wreck the car. Teens simply do not anticipate trouble when they cut across the corner gas station lot to beat the light. Shaving thirty seconds off their drive time seems to make sense, and it would have, if that old guy had looked where he was going.

We can substitute a Pandora's box of trouble for "wreck the car" in that scenario: They could try unprotected sex; they could try a drink handed to them by a stranger; they could, they could, they could. Teens define risk differently than their parents do. Inside the adolescent brain, there is little to worry about.

As parents we face an existential conundrum: We are trying to communicate with sentient beings whose crania contain different machinery than ours do. Anyone who has tried and failed to keep the dog off the bed knows that it is hard to bridge that kind of equipment gap, particularly when desire is in play. Our dog stays off the couch when we are around, but we know, from the hair, the heat, and the paw prints, that she hops up as soon as we turn our backs. She would use the television remote control if she could work the buttons. She would eat all the cheese in the refrigerator if she could pull on the handle hard enough — not to be rebellious but because it seemed like a very good idea at the time. Even a dog knows that authority does not always survive separation.

Identity Crises

"I SEE SOMETHING NEW."

Harry made this announcement every couple of months; since he did not see Sarah every day, he prided himself on noting the larger changes in her life. We were distracted by minutiae, but not Harry, who saw it as his godfatherly duty to put things into perspective for us. His most recent appraisal came after dinner at a Chinese restaurant — the last item on our family's early-bird social agenda and the first stop in a night of club hopping for him and Judith — and as we walked to the car, he pulled me aside.

Her hand gestures had changed, he said, and so had her voice. He was right. When she was little, her hands had a life of their own, wandering off into space with no more purpose than to feel the air pass by. Now she talked with her hands — upturned palms to express bewilderment, palms down, cutting the air on a horizontal plane, to make a point. Her voice was smoother than it used to be, having lost the double-tone wobble that used to amuse us. I pointed out that her hair had gotten thicker. The weight of it had turned her ringlets into waves.

I wanted to know what Harry made of all this.

"I can see the teenager coming," he said, without an inch of malice. "Kiss her good-bye."

A FEW NIGHTS LATER she was gone, unexpectedly, a last-minute sleepover. My first thought was that there was no need to cook dinner, so we got the last containers of sushi at the fish market, which we could eat with last night's pizza, in bed, while we watched a rented movie. There would still be time for sex, to say nothing of tomorrow morning's crossword puzzle.

If we were dating, an agenda like that would border on insult. Under the circumstances, it sounded like a dream. Perception was everything: This was not a hodgepodge pickup meal; this was fusion cuisine.

We had eaten and settled in with the movie when Larry was betrayed by the tiniest snore. I understood, I really did. In addition to working, he tried hard to live up to his preschool reputation as a "participatory dad," which meant that he showed up from time to time and knew the teachers' names. I used to wonder, loudly, at the inequity of it all — how come he got so much attention for stuff that moms did all the time? I stopped caring long ago. Let people sing his praises, as long as he helped clean up after dinner and carried the laundry downstairs.

Of course he fell asleep. He got up before I did in the morning, to walk the dog. It was only natural that he should be ready for dreamland before I was.

Tough.

I elbowed him in the side, harder than was absolutely necessary, and he snapped to attention the same way he did when I woke him, years ago, to announce that there was a burglar in the house.

"What?"

"You have to figure out how not to fall asleep," I said, "because we're going to have lots of nights together after Sarah's gone. We could watch movies and talk about them. We could do things."

He gave me a wary look.

"I do not want to spend those nights alone while you're asleep," I said.

After all, this was the relationship that would last, in terms of nuts-and-bolts daily life. We would be Sarah's parents forever, but that was no guarantee of proximity, not the way a marriage was. For the last eleven years, we had been mostly a family. As she got older, we would be mostly a couple again, and we had to be prepared. I have read conflicting articles about who has the worst time when a child leaves home — some experts say it is the full-time moms, who feel as adrift as their own mothers had, and others say it is the hard-line careerists, both men and women, who regret having missed so much of their kids' childhood. One way to interpret the findings is that everyone has trouble adjusting, if all they have left is a void.

The American Psychiatric Association officially retired the phrase *empty nest* in 1980, citing a bias among male therapists who failed to understand that some women were thrilled by their newly independent lives. But change is change, no matter what they call it, and I want to be prepared. It struck me that Larry and I would do a better job of letting Sarah go if we had a plan for ourselves that involved something more compelling than falling asleep with the television on.

* * *

WE HEARD REPORTS that the latest beachfront hotel was swankier than anything else on the Santa Monica strip, so the next time we had the baby-sitter, Larry and I decided to walk down to see for ourselves. We did not last long. The bar was full of sleek people under thirty, possessed of equally sleek little flip-phones on which they were having urgent conversations. Everyone wore black and had a disaffected air; everyone had the kind of pouty mouth that in ten years would require one of those new plumping cosmetics, if not the contents of a syringe. We couldn't have been more out of place if we were wearing plastic badges from a PTA convention, so we slunk over to the adjacent hotel, where the hip quotient was lower. There was a couple with a stroller at the next table, which made us feel much better. We fit right in.

A WEEK LATER we went to a party at Harry and Judith's house, where I inadvertently made a fashion statement by being the only female guest whose pants had a normal waistband. Harry and Larry are contemporaries, but I was about Sarah's age when Judith was born, which means that we appreciate each other's sense of style and would never want to borrow an outfit. Her friends shared her flair for — how shall I say it? — dramatic attire. Two of them introduced me to a third woman and called me elegant, which might have been an apologetic reference to the waistband, and articulate, which I believed to be code for out-of-it. No point in talking to me about the newest band at the newest club, and watch out if I reached into my bag for that brag book full of photos.

If I sound a bit defensive, it is because I felt that way. I had temporarily lost what sociologists would call my cohort — my affinity group, the demographic sliver that felt familiar to me. Among the hip single professionals, I stuck out like an unmanicured thumb, but I did not care for the prevailing middle-age stereotypes — neither the stick figure who fled advancing age on silly shoes nor the diffident matron who inspired even her contemporaries to call her "ma'am." My job didn't sound like real work to women in power offices, but it sounded like way too much to do to women like my school pal, Lori. I was temporarily at sea.

The world sometimes made a choice for me. An Italian friend had warned me that I would be invisible on the trip we took with Harry and Judith and Rosetta the writing bear; everyone would notice Sarah, because she was a child, and Judith, because she was blond. "You," he said, wanting to prepare me, "will just be the *mamma.*" He was right. I did not care for that role either.

I WAS PREOCCUPIED when we got home from the party, and I tucked Sarah into bed with more focus on the product — a sleeping child, it was so late — than on the process. I did not hear her say that she loved me, so I said good night and gave her a kiss. My exit line was, "Get some sleep now."

The next morning she said that her feelings were hurt because I had not told her that I loved her.

"Hey, someday you'll be in love with someone," I said, "and after years of being together you'll say, 'I love you,' and he'll say, 'Pass the mustard.'"

"He isn't my mother," she shot back.

SARAH AND HER SCHOOLMATE Katie spent a day visiting the girls' school they had applied to, and an English teacher asked them what the worst thing was about girls their age. Katie piped up, "They tell secrets behind each other's backs."

Sarah told me this after her Saturday riding lesson, over a chicken sandwich at a local outdoor café. And then, out of nowhere, she confided that she was having trouble fitting in this year. Julia had a new best friend who in turn had access to the cool crowd, and suddenly her friendship with Sarah was relegated to the bench — just as good as ever, but only when the other girls were not around. Sarah was not exactly sure what to do.

It was a good meal for a confessional — between the dripping barbecue sauce and the dipping of french fries into ketchup, there was very little opportunity for eye contact. Once she made the initial disclosure, the rest came pouring out. Lots of the girls wanted to pair up with a best friend, and they didn't want a third wheel. The cool group, a constellation of best friends, had room for Sarah, but she did not have the price of admission, which included an interest in either Britney Spears or boys, or both. Julia's musical tastes were far too eclectic to tolerate Britney, whom she disdained, but she qualified by virtue of having that other girlfriend as well as friends who were boys. In fact, part of Sarah's frustration stemmed from the fact that Julia wasn't a typical cool girl at all, and yet she had gained admission to their crowd, while Sarah had not.

A couple of the decidedly uncool girls were all over Sarah like puppies on a shoe, but she wasn't interested in them either. It had nothing to do with who was in or out. Sarah wanted to be able to float for a while longer. She had known most of these girls since kindergarten, and the sudden boundaries made little sense to her.

No matter. Girls paired off, and Sarah paid for not having done so. The impenetrable geometry of sixth grade made her feel lonely for the first time in her life.

So did I want some more fries, and what should she do?

I didn't know. Sirens and bells went off in my brain: This was our first big adolescent-issue conversation, not a mere matter of weekend logistics or homework assignments or outgrown clothes. She had chosen me as her confidante, and I had no idea what to say. In third grade I hit a girl who reneged on a promise to walk home from school with me instead of with the crowd who lived a half block in the other direction. In eighth grade I was summarily dismissed from the vinyl-purse clique by girls who decided that anyone who had glasses and braces and no breasts lacked sufficient cachet. My résumé was pathetic, and my daughter was waiting for me to say something.

I told her that Julia would always be her friend, even if they end up living across the world from each other.

I told her she was right — she didn't have much in common with the cool girls.

I told her that the uncool girls were really interesting kids, but I understood the business about not wanting to be overwhelmed.

I said I understood her frustration about everyone pairing off.

From the look on her face, I could tell what she was thinking:

If this is the best mom can do, I could eat by myself and not have to share the fries.

When I had a problem with a friend, my parents used to interrogate me about what I had done to warrant rejection, which was not a confidence builder. But there was no one to blame in Sarah's story. This was preclique behavior, the pairing up of girls so that each member of the duo felt better about herself: A girl who had a best friend must be someone special, because someone special always had a best friend. The very act of shutting other girls out elevated the status of the girls who did the shutting. Duos were the farm team; girls who showed a talent for exclusivity would someday graduate to larger cliques.

Understanding the source of Sarah's distress would not necessarily make her feel better, though. If only I were a better listener — the type who could elicit information with an understanding nod and help a girl find the solution herself. When the curriculum director at Sarah's school told a sixth grader, "There are certainly a lot of things changing this year," it was like flipping a switch: No matter whom she talked to, the child inevitably wanted to talk back. When Larry or I said something like that, we sounded as if we were reciting an exercise from the empathy handbook. Worse, Sarah knew it. She would roll those big eyes of hers as if to say, "Can't you do any better than that?"

Possibly not. Modulated was not a word anyone ever used to describe either Larry or me, and at a difficult moment like this, I saw everything I could not fix in myself reflected back with terrible clarity. Skin as thin as a head of garlic's had its advantages — I liked to think it enhanced life's good times — but it made the darker moments feel like a root canal without Novocain. I hated every girl who had ever turned her back on a friend, just to be able to do so, but the last thing Sarah needed was a nasty, backbiting shrew for a mother.

I devoutly believed that Sarah would survive and that after a while it would all get better. I did not want to dignify the miasma of girl gossip and snubs by taking it too seriously, but I could not insult Sarah by acting as though her feelings were not worthy of consideration. There was no good way to parse cliques. All the advice in the world was useless when a girl felt bad. Worse than useless, because it set a mom apart, in the vague, pontificating distance.

Then it struck me that Sarah might not want advice at all. The one thing I knew, that she didn't, was what awaited her on the far side of cliques. I was an adult with friends, and I could talk to her about that. So I told her the truth, which was that I made my best friends after I got out of college, for reasons I still did not understand. One friend was not yet forty and had a hot date last weekend, and one was close to seventy and baby-sat her grandson once a week. Then there was Judith, who lived a half mile away and had enough leather pants to upholster a herd of cattle, and Ginger, who lived in New York and spent last year banking her latte money to see how much she could save. There was time, and space, for all kinds of friendship.

Sarah seemed to like that idea. Adolescence may feel like a revolution to parents, but it veered close to fascism for the girls. I could not fix things for her, but I could remind her, with some credibility, that there were lots of ways out.

JULIA'S MOM, PHYLLIS, was educated by the nuns and thought that the exclamation "Jesus, Mary, and Joseph!" was potent stuff. I grew up in a Jewish suburb and went through a phase when I used obscenities as adjectives, just to show that I could. Phyllis had worked her whole life for a nonprofit foundation; my only experience with nonprofit was inadvertent, when I spent too much time on a project and netted about twelve cents an hour. But we had one crucial thing in common — a deep if misplaced faith in academics, a belief peculiar to women who grew up in the sixties and seventies. We agreed that a girl's brain mattered more than a boy's did, because a woman still had to elbow her way into rooms primarily occupied by men. She ought to be overqualified, to compensate for a lingering gender disadvantage, at least in some fields. We considered sloth to be the deadliest of the seven sins.

We were slightly out of touch, since the world was full of people who had never bothered with a second draft of that history report and were doing just fine. No matter. We wanted our girls to persevere at school and we wanted them to take themselves seriously. We each wanted to raise a hardworking daughter who might — Jesus, Mary, and Joseph! — clean up her room, in Julia's case, or write a thank-you note before she outgrew the gift, in Sarah's.

Between Phyllis's work schedule and mine, we were lucky to have lunch twice each school year, and in the name of efficiency, it was always the same frantic deal: We met at a dim sum place that was close to her office, where we could point at the dishes we wanted without having to interrupt ourselves. There was no time to listen to a list of today's specials; we had a lot to cover in one hour.

Especially today: Phyllis reported that Julia had discovered instant messaging and was part of an information tribe that included boys. Julia knew the plotline of *Gilmore Girls* and had lots of weekend plans with her friends. I said that Sarah forgot to check her e-mail for weeks at a time and thought that most of the boys in her class were an unwanted distraction. We taped *The West Wing* to watch on the weekends, and her favorite character was the White House press secretary.

Each of the girls seemed perfectly happy, and somewhere between the third and fourth round of shu mai, the truth hit us: They were more different from each other than they had been a year ago, probably less different than they would be by the time they started seventh grade. No way we could have predicted it, and nothing we could do about it, except to stand nearby and wait to see what happened next.

LIKE ANYONE WHOSE FRAME is smaller than her ambitions, I liked suit jackets, which were the best possible defense against diminishing adjectives like the dread "petite." In the waning days of collective sanity, before the middle school acceptance or rejection letters arrived, the principal scheduled a special evening for sixth-grade parents. I figured a substantial jacket would make me feel stronger, so I grabbed an ancient black-and-white tweed and stood in front of the mirror, checking for moth holes. Sarah gave me the once-over.

"I really, really like that jacket," she said. "A lot."

I took it off and handed it to her.

"Why don't you try it on?"

She grabbed it in case I was going to change my mind, put it on over her sweatshirt, and stood in front of the mirror.

"If it was my size and the shoulders were a little smaller, I could wear a jacket like this," she said. I stepped up behind her, like a tailor, and pushed the shoulders into line.

"I like it long," she said, a good thing, since it hung almost to her knees. "Do you like it long?"

"I do," I said.

She smiled at the mirror and turned sideways, and to the front again, in no hurry to give back my jacket. I could point out that I'd be late for the meeting, but that seemed as rude as a loud alarm clock. This was not a little girl's dress-up. This was Sarah trying on her next self, after the shifting social alliances had settled, after grades and tests and all the instability that came with change. I wanted her to know that everything she imagined when she put on that jacket was true. And I was grateful that she had seen something she wanted to borrow, when I had it on.

So I waited for her to be done, and then I said, "Y'know, I think you're going to be a jacket girl."

14

Faith

IT WAS LITTLE MORE THAN A CRAVING FOR BRISKET THAT LED me to give my first Passover seder seventeen years ago, but I failed to take the yearnings of other wandering Jews into account. Over the years, the event outgrew our dining room chairs and even the backup silverware. We rented tables and invited nonbelievers who were willing to endure an abridged service for the chance to have dinner with friends. On one night each spring, we got to see everyone we cared for and didn't see enough of during the rest of the year.

For the first six years, there were no children. Now we had Sarah, Aviva, Emily and her older sister, Julia and her younger, a girl from across town, the boy whose family invited us over for Christmas dinner, and Laura and David's son. Finally we had what every seder was supposed to have — children to read the four questions that explained just how lucky our ancestors had been.

And we had ritual, even if some of it was mere logistics. We banished the living room furniture to the front bedroom to make room for the rented tables and chairs. We had flowers and place cards and table linens, and we had a list of imperatives, the things we had to have to make the evening ours: Laura always brought homemade chopped liver, everyone told her it was the best they had ever tasted, and she apologized that the secret ingredient was Miracle Whip; the brisket was my Grandma Ethel's recipe; Carolyn brought strawberries and purposely forgot to take her serving bowl home, as though that guaranteed us another year together; one friend brought the asparagus; and one picked up the same array of desserts, year in and year out, on her way over to our house. These were our small eternities. We depended on them.

This year Emily and her sister recited the four questions in Hebrew, and Sarah and the other girls shared them in English. There was no miracle here — words gave up their mystery with a fair ease once a girl was eleven — but the grown-ups listened with a hushed respect. Girls we had known since they were babies asked ancient questions, and grandparents recalled the dinner table full of ghosts where they had asked the same questions long ago. Time fell away.

This was our congregation: thirty-five people who rushed over straight from work or spent the day cooking, who grabbed their kids from school and insisted on nice clothes, who every year uttered the prayer "Next year, in Israel," when what we really hoped for was another year to get together and exclaim over how the children had grown.

There was nothing remarkable about any of it, except that we had been together for seventeen years, in a city where the half-life of a starlet was seventeen months. Every year the seder reminded us to pay attention to all the things that were hard to articulate without sounding like a sap. We had children who spoke, and read, and ransacked the house, crazy with laughter, looking for a hidden piece of matzo. We were blessed.

WHEN I WAS LITTLE I heard a lot about God's omnipotence, but instead of feeling reassured, I felt stifled. Wasn't there any way to step out of his line of sight? One night I began my usual dental ritual, toothbrush in the right hand, tube of toothpaste in the left. I squirted a half inch onto the brush and turned on the faucet — and then I threw the brush into the sink and ran out of the room.

I stood in the hallway, breathless and triumphant. God had thought I was going to brush my teeth, but at the last moment I had thrown him a curve. I was free. I was my own girl.

The voice of faith replied, "Foolish girl. He knew you were going to drop the brush before you did."

There was no way out. I came to resist organized religion, in the same way a teen might resist a domineering parent. When the rabbi asked the members of my high school confirmation class if anyone still doubted the existence of God, I defiantly raised my hand — not because I doubted the existence of God but because I rejected the rabbi's smugness. I believed devoutly in the restorative power of the holiday dinner, but I had a lot of trouble with the institution.

I had read that children who had a religious upbringing were less likely to get into trouble as teens. Being on God's team was as important as having a sport, so I tried, I did. When Sarah was in the third grade, I surrendered to my self-doubt, overruled Larry's indifference, and signed her up at a religious school. They swore that they had room for a child who would not be bat mitzvahed. She could be confirmed without having to learn Hebrew; she could find out about Jewish ethics and religion, history and culture, without the ceremonial formalities.

No one informed the Hebrew teacher of our priorities, though. She berated Sarah for not knowing any Hebrew and urged her to work harder so that she could catch up with the students on the bat mitzvah track. She dismissed as a pale excuse from an unwilling worker Sarah's explanation that she was not going to be bat mitzvahed. This woman of God made Sarah cry, a feat no teacher had accomplished before or since, and so we took her out of religious school.

After that we settled for a seder, a Hanukkah party at our house, and a serious family conversation on the Day of Atonement about how each one of us might behave better in the coming year. My mother frequently reminded me that we had failed our child by not worshiping in a more traditional fashion. I thought what I have always thought: Faith may enjoy a congregation, but it does not require a bureaucracy.

A COUPLE OF NIGHTS after the seder, *Out of Africa* was on one of the four thousand cable channels we seem to get, and I was so pleased to have stumbled upon something I liked that I started to watch, even though it was two-thirds over. When Larry fell into bed, he reached for the remote control to surf, as men tend to do, since as far as I can tell they actually prefer to watch television in three-second bits. I yelped, and he grudgingly went back to the movie.

"You like sad stories," he said, in the hope that to prove him wrong I would let him change the channel.

"I do," I said. "No, actually, I like stories where I end up thinking, 'But what if you'd done this instead of that?'" Like an overzealous graduate student, I launched into a list of irreversible moments in fiction — in *Appointment in Samarra, House of Mirth,*

Madame Bovary, The Great Gatsby. The older Sarah got, the more I fixated on the consequences of seemingly inconsequential events. Any mother with even a moment for self-reflection considered the things she did or said that she would like to take back and could not, the comments that might change the course of history with her daughter. I had my father's short fuse and fought hard to control it, but I fully expected to put my foot in my mouth as Sarah grew older. I prayed that she would forgive me — or better, that she would know when to ignore me. In the meantime, I laid a proprietary hand on top of the remote control so that I could watch Meryl Streep suffer through venereal disease and Robert Redford's commitment issues without interruption.

TALK ABOUT TRADITION: Parents of older children warned us that school letters still arrived in a fat envelope, if it was good news, or a thin one, since it took very little space to say, No, you may not come to our school. Bruce the mailman knew weeks in advance that the letters were supposed to go out on March 25, since he had been delivering the future for years. He could walk the streets and rattle off whose kid was at which school, from elementary school straight through college. He had seen his share of frantic parents standing expectantly at the front door, and when he could, he jiggered his route to get them their mail first.

He promised us, and he promised Julia's folks, that he would start with us on the day the letters came — which he did, except that it was two days earlier than we had expected. I was not waiting for him. I was wasting my time window-shopping, waiting for Sarah's Saturday-morning drama class to end, when my cell phone rang.

"The envelopes arrived," Larry said. "Bruce brought them before he started the route."

"Fat or thin?"

"What?"

"Are the envelopes big or little?"

"There's more than one. Let's see. Two little ones and one big one."

Sarah had applied to only two schools, so why did we have three envelopes?

"No, wait, there's one on the stoop I didn't see," Larry said. "Two big and two small."

"Where are they from?"

One big and one small from each of the schools.

Two big envelopes. I stood in a doorway to block out the traffic noise, and I called the front-row moms, who had already opened their mail. This year, just to drive parents mad, there was a small variation on the usual theme — the thin envelopes held the formal acceptance or rejection letters, and the fat ones held all the forms a new student had to fill out. Everybody's girl had gotten in to every school, and it was a good bet they would end up choosing the same one. Good news all around — the girls would have old friends to offset the strangeness of a new school, and the parents would have old friends to accompany us one more step into the future.

Sarah had a choice, even though she already knew where she wanted to go, and it was the choice that made me happy for her. In the coming days I would hear stories of girls who struggled to make their second choice feel like the best thing and of startled boys who had no choice at all. Parents begged schools to reconsider, and children who should have thought only of graduation harbored instead a dark sense that they had come up short. We had skated by. Sarah would be that much older before she faced whatever the first big disappointment of her life turned out to be.

* * *

SARAH COULD HAVE CALLED the girls on my cell phone as we drove home, but she wanted to savor the news before she did — and she wanted to see Larry before she shared it with anyone else. It was a vestigial bit of childhood loyalty: Good news required acknowledgment from both parents before it was officially, absolutely good news.

Then she sprawled on the couch and called the girls, looking for all the world like — well, like a teenager. At the start of the year, the principal had told us that the kids would be chafing at the bit by the time the letters came out, ready to move on, and we had laughed, because the girls loved that school so much. We could not imagine them being impatient to leave.

So much for our imagination.

A couple of nights later, I dreamed that Sarah was taller than I was.

15
Fashion

IT WAS ONE OF THOSE SPRING DAYS IN MANHATTAN THAT make people forget what the city is like in August or when it snows too hard or when a bicycle messenger decides to play chicken with a pack of pedestrians. The breeze was a happy descant of cool air, and everyone was on the street at lunchtime, including Sarah and me, on our way to grab a sausage sandwich from a highly recommended street vendor and then to meet Larry.

We were moving toward the intersection, arm in arm, Sarah on my left, when a voice behind me, to my right, made an appreciative comment about my ass. In the split second before I turned to see who he was, I had several simultaneous thoughts:

How dare he? I was an upstanding career woman in my dress-for-success clothes, and my anatomy was my business, thank you.

How dare he within earshot of my daughter, who luckily had just spotted our lunch destination and clearly did not hear him.

And then indignation stepped aside, so that wistful could have her say: When was the last time that a man other than my husband said anything more enthusiastic to me than "Nice glasses. Where'd you get the frames?"

Right before I turned around, I prayed that he was not an obvious psycho. I glanced back. All the men within a radius of ten feet looked fairly normal. What a relief — in a profound and politically incorrect kind of way.

THE LATEST TREND in women's wardrobes is what comic Janeane Garofolo derisively calls "thong feminism" because it seems to confuse exposure with liberation. The thinking goes like this: A truly independent woman wears whatever she damn pleases because she is so comfortable in her own skin, so very proud of her physical form. An independent woman works hard on her body, as a matter not of vanity but of self-respect, and she is not shy about showing it off. At the vanguard of the movement are members of the radical fringe, who wear revealing clothes without bothering to work on their biceps or their glutes, but that is because they are highly evolved, or can't live without chocolate, or both.

The problem with the newest iteration of women's lib is that it ignores a dynamic known to any woman who has ever drawn a stare on the sidewalk: Lots of men have yet to embrace any kind of feminism, be it first-wave, second-wave, or thong. As long as a new teen singing sensation hits the market every six months, wearing outfits that scream "sex object," women run the risk of being misunderstood. A scantily clad girl is not an emblem of power and autonomy, not to everyone. To some portion of the male viewing public, she is an animated photo spread. Thong feminism might seem like liberation to women who have not yet voted for president, but to conspiracy theorists it looks more like a successful campaign by retailers and the media to keep women looking like boy toys. It is exhibitionism repackaged to look like freedom by savvy capitalists who know that sex sells.

I would not suggest for a moment that women ought to cover up to keep men from thinking lascivious thoughts. I think a woman ought to wear whatever she wants to wear. The question is not whether we should pick out our own clothes. The question is why a woman wants to wear a pink G-string, with the straps hiked to stick out above jeans that barely cover her pubic bone, in the first place.

My friends and I were as guilty, in our day, of using attire to express attitude. If women had invested all the money we saved not buying bras, we would be far closer to retirement than we are. The other contingent, the women who stormed the professional workplace, proved only that we could dress in as boring a fashion as our male counterparts did. One group dressed to break out and the other to break in, but at least we had a political agenda beyond showing skin. I am not sure that underwear as outerwear qualifies as social dogma.

But it is the dominant model, and some of my wearier contemporaries have decided to get with the program. One mother espouses a tidy piece of thong revisionism: Her daughter has too strong a sense of self to settle for clothes that don't draw attention. Supergirls do not hide their light under a bushel or their cleavage under a shirt that fits. This mom admitted that she hates most of the clothing in question, but endorsement was a far easier position to take than disapproval, which led only to arguments in dressing rooms and mall parking lots.

One marketing expert suggests that parents yield on clothing issues to save their ammunition for bigger battles on drugs and sex, but that seemed counterintuitive to me. If I'm thirteen and I've just talked my mom into an outfit that makes me look like Jodie Foster in *Taxi Driver,* why would I bother to ask her blessing on activities that skirt the letter of the law? Mom is a marshmallow. No need to consult her any further.

Braniff airlines strutted through the marketplace in 1967 with the advertising slogan "When you've got it, flaunt it" and went out of business fifteen years later. I bet that fifteen years from now, about the time that gravity consigns their perkiness to the past tense, the thong feminists will conveniently discover the error of their ways and decide that inner beauty is what really matters.

CLOTHES WERE ON MY MIND because Sarah and I had set aside a whole day to look for a graduation dress. Another girl from school happened to be in New York with her mom, so the four of us planned a classic mother-and-daughter retail outing, starting with brunch and ending, we were sure, with two perfect dresses.

It was not going to be easy. Roberta's daughter, Ellie, was a full head taller than Sarah and already had a figure, so our efforts had to take in both ends of the tween spectrum — the junior department, where Roberta hoped to find an appropriately modest dress, and the children's department, which with any luck would have dresses that did not look like they belonged to children.

We had not taken into account the cultural differences between Manhattan, where people still got dressed up for parties, and Los Angeles, where an invitation that required "casual evening wear" was little more than a request to leave the flip-flops at home. The first children's store we tried had at least twenty dresses in

Sarah's size, each one a variation on a single theme — a tight bodice and short sleeves atop a poufy skirt, in pale colors and whisper fabrics. I swooned and tried to hide it. I made my mother's speech about things looking different on people than they did on the hanger. Sarah refused even to try one on.

We went to a store for Ellie next, full of dresses that were, Sarah confessed, "exactly what I would like," long, simple sleeveless dresses in a springtime assortment of floral patterns. Ever helpful, Roberta found the smallest size and held it up to Sarah: no deal. Ellie, who had empathy to spare, announced that she could go shopping at home, she didn't need to try anything on, or maybe just one, if Sarah didn't mind waiting.

But Sarah insisted that Ellie try on lots of dresses. She buzzed around the store, looking for new patterns in Ellie's size, and whenever she found one, she brought it to the fitting room, knocked on the door, and held it up for her friend's perusal. She asked the saleswoman for help, and she gave Ellie her considered opinion on every single dress. She created the experience she had wanted to have, and could not have, and gave it to someone else.

A WEEK LATER her dress found us as surely as if it had a voice to call my name. It beckoned from the end of a rack at a store that happened to be between a doctor's appointment and an errand: a dress and coat that combined everything Sarah liked; tiny mauve and lilac flowers sprinkled on raw silk that wasn't ivory and wasn't pink, and a boat neck, whose allure had something to do with Audrey Hepburn in *Funny Face.* I took home the size Sarah wore and one size bigger, just in case, wishing that she had been with me so that it would have felt more like her choice.

I tried for an offhand mood.

"Look, I saw a dress today you might like; actually it's a dress with a coat, and . . ."

"Did you buy it?"

"Well, I brought it home. We can always return . . ."

"Where is it?"

"Are your hands clean?"

"*Mom.*"

She disappeared into her bedroom with the outfit, which gave me just enough time to holler down to Larry to come upstairs. We stood like idiots, and we waited.

She stepped into the hallway with such dignity — Sarah, the young lady on the brink. Miraculously, I did not burst into tears. I had magic eyes: I could see forward, to Sarah at her high school graduation, in college, on her wedding day. I had a glimpse of her coming into her own.

A long time ago, out of nowhere, I had told her that a dress did not make a girl beautiful. It was the other way around.

"What a lucky outfit," I managed. "You make it look wonderful."

She stood in front of the mirror, and spun, and wondered aloud if she could get shoes that weren't as flat as a pancake.

"We'll go shopping," I said.

SARAH'S SCHOOL USED TO HAVE grandparents' day, until the realities of today's families required a change of name, to grandparents' and special friends' day. Between divorce, later pregnancies, and the diaspora that had separated my generation from our parents, there simply weren't as many available grandparents as there used to be, and a large portion of the student body had no one to bring. The special friends category allowed for a bigger celebration.

The day was important to Sarah, who had only one surviving grandparent, and to my mother, whose other two grandchildren were already in college. They shared lunch on the playground, and then they headed back to the classroom for a project the teacher had planned. Each child was going to interview her grandparent or special friend, using questions the children had drawn up in advance.

They sat in three-quarter-size chairs, and Sarah took out her paper and pencil.

"What are your most important memories?" was her first question.

"When I was twelve," my mother said, "I went to my grandparents' fiftieth wedding anniversary, and it was a big party. I remember I got to wear a fancy dress and special fancy ankle socks. And I remember my own parents' fiftieth wedding anniversary because we had a party for them in our backyard. And I remember marrying Grandpa Ira, and your mom and your aunt being born."

Sarah wondered if there was anything more recent.

"No," said my mother. After a moment, she said, "That's enough memories," and they talked about something else.

Sarah repeated this conversation again and again once she got home, and the following afternoon she presented her analysis over an after-school snack.

"I think the reason she said 'That's enough memories' is because her life now isn't as interesting as her life was then. I'm sorry to say that, but it's what I think."

Of course it was true; how could it not be? My parents got married when my dad was twenty-one and my mother was nineteen, and they stayed married for forty-four years, until death did them part. They had picked out a southern California retirement community with a golf course so they could be near the kids and grandkids and the putting green. That was the plan, until the internist called to say there was something he was sure was scar tissue on my dad's X rays.

Ira was not a gullible fellow. "If it's scar tissue," he replied, "how come it was never there before?"

God reached down, erased the family equation, and wrote a new one in its place. A few years later my mother married Allen, whose wife had died six months before my father did — and yet none of his life with my mother had made the memory list at school.

"I think you're right, honey, but I think it's the same for Allen," I said. "Most of their life was with their families, and now that's over. This is a new part of their lives, and it's interesting, but it's so different. I think Grandma said 'That's enough memories' because she didn't want to get sad in front of you."

Out of nowhere — okay, out of the guilt I still felt about not letting my mom join us in Italy — I floated the idea that we could take a more manageable trip. We could take Grandma to New York. That very morning she had mentioned that the last time she was there was to visit Memorial Sloan-Kettering Cancer Center with my dad. She'd like to go back, but Allen wasn't much interested in the idea.

With genuine bewilderment, Sarah wondered why she didn't go herself.

"She doesn't know her way around the city," I explained, "and besides, she would be afraid to be on the street in the evening by herself."

"I'm not afraid in New York," Sarah announced.

"Well, Grandma has led a more sheltered life than you have, and she'd be anxious. You have me and Daddy to help you get around."

"I could hail a cab." She shot her arm in the air and waggled her fingertips.

I was irked at her unwillingness to acknowledge my mom's limitations, even though we had worked hard to convince her that people could do whatever they set their minds to do.

"I just think that before she gets to be a little old lady, there are some things it would be nice to do," I said.

"You don't think she's a little old lady now?"

"No," I said, emphatically. "I don't think she's a little old lady."

WE TOOK THE DRESS AND COAT to Gary the tailor, who had been downsizing clothes for me for more than twenty years. I did not know his wife's name, and he did not know where I lived, but we knew everything about each other's daughters. I knew where his two girls had gone to high school and college, and about the marriage proposal the older one turned down. I knew he couldn't go for a month without seeing them. He knew — he told me this every time he saw me — that Sarah was a good student and a wonderful girl. He often reminded Larry that it would be his job to fight off the unacceptable beaus. We doted, he and I, together.

With a mouthful of straight pins, he marveled at how quickly we had arrived at elementary school graduation. He pinned the hems and tapered the coat, just a little, and then he refused to give me a bill. "No, I cannot charge you for this," he said. "I love this girl. Sarah, may I have a hug and a kiss?"

One of the lessons of preschool was that hugs and kisses belonged to the person who bestowed them, and Sarah, who was reserved about her affections, had driven her share of relatives and friends crazy, over the years, by preferring to shake hands. She did it to keep her distance. But this time she stepped forward, kissed Gary on the cheek, and whispered, "Thank you."

He made us promise to bring in a photograph. "You must take a lot of them, because this is so important," he said. "I still look at my old photos from time to time, but it's hard, because they make me cry."

I had known Gary for more than ten years before I found out how he adored his daughters, and had I never had a child, I might never have known.

I had spent most of my adult life on the other side, happy to be childless, so much time that I could never be one of those proselytizers who insisted that children made us whole. I didn't think that — or I did for us but not for everyone. I wished for a truce between people with children and people without, just as I wished for it between women who made money and those who did not. The last-minute mother saw both sides: The absolute insignificance, and the crystalline delight, of yet another kid dressed up for graduation.

SOMEWHERE I READ that the designer Vera Wang held an annual sample sale of her bridal gowns in a Manhattan hotel. On a single day, gowns that a normal person could not afford were within the reach of the bride-to-be, as long as she was willing to get up at the crack of dawn, stand in line, and peel to her underwear in front of strangers to try on a dress. Given the stripping, the sale was for women only. Future husbands and fathers of the bride had to settle for a cell phone play-by-play.

There were years between now and then, possibly decades, and Sarah's prospective husband might have a mother who had waited all that time for the chance to unpack her mother's antique gown. Reality could get in our way, down the line, but no matter. I suggested to Sarah that we might visit that sale, someday, and she jumped at the chance.

"Could we stay at that hotel the night before?"

"I guess so."

"If we did we could get up early and get right in line."

"That's true."

"Good," she said. "Let's do that, okay?"

There. We had a date, as though we were going tomorrow.

16

Plot Twists

ROCKY THE QUARTER HORSE WAS THE SIZE OF A FAMILY VAN, but we had no choice. The pony Sarah had been leasing got sold, and his very cautious new owner refused to let him jump. With an only child's fervor, Sarah wanted to ride in the school equestrian league when she got to seventh grade; she had no idea what a horse show was like, but she knew she wanted teammates, and we wanted her to have them. So we shifted her over to Rocky, a big guy with a big guy's distaste for having the saddle put on and the girth fastened tight enough to keep it there. For the first time, I got a little nervous. She looked like a gnat on an elephant. The first commandment of rider stability, "wrap your legs around him," was a joke. She might as well clamp tight to a beer barrel.

But Meredith approved. "She looks good on that big horse," she said, as Sarah entered the ring. Later in the lesson, she observed that Sarah seemed a more aggressive rider than she had been on the pony, which was a good thing.

All I thought was, Be careful what you wish for. "Aggressive" was not an adjective that anyone had ever before used to describe Sarah.

AT DINNER SARAH ANNOUNCED, "I already wrote my graduation essay."

I had written it too, in my head, a draft in which she thanked me for having read to her almost every night of her life, between the ages of six weeks and six years. All the other mothers would regard me with admiration, not envy, because they knew I deserved the recognition. Sarah thanked Larry for something, too, but I didn't fantasize about what it was because this was my daydream. I just wanted her to talk about family.

"Want to read it for us?" I asked.

"Mom, you know I can't."

Of course I knew. The whole point was that the graduation speech was her first completely independent work. We missed seeing some homework assignments because we didn't have the time or interest or inclination to take a look, but that was our choice. This time it was hers. The school encouraged the divorce: The teachers explicitly instructed the kids not to share even the first draft.

They did not take into account the finely honed interrogative skills of the working journalist. I could ask a trap question with the best of them.

"Did you spell Bella's name right?"

I despised myself.

"Oh, none of the family's in it."

So much for the heart-wrenching thanks to mom, who made up all those stories about the Wicked Queen and the starfish jewel, who sang "Good Night, Ladies" at bedtime to everyone we knew or wanted to know, who let her wear any color combination she wanted, even when my family was around.

Stop it. Public adulation was never part of the bargain.

During my own extended tenure at religious school, I learned that there were eight levels of *tzedakah,* or charity, and the anonymous gift had greater merit than the one that came with a credit line. Naming rights were for lesser mortals, who wouldn't do good unless they got attention for it. In the same way, the highest form of motherhood seemed to be invisibility. All those books and stories we had read were in Sarah's pores, and that was that.

I had been no different when I was her age. Aside from the predictable breakfast constellation of cold cereal set out at the six o'clock position, orange juice at eleven and milk at one, I had little memory of what my mother did for me in junior high and high school. To be honest, I could not have cared less, since the vivid part of my life was in front of me. The hardest thing about having an adolescent daughter was remembering how I had played her part: with a cut-and-run indifference, with an eye toward getting out. My parents were peripheral to the real story of my life — perfectly tolerable, compared with the overtly awful ones I knew, but beside the point.

"Is it poignant? Is it funny? Will I cry?"

"Maybe," she said.

PUBERTY WASN'T THE ONLY THING that hit girls earlier these days. In the waning weeks of sixth grade, Sarah and her pals developed a pretty good case of senioritis. They were all going to the same girls' school next year, so their academic future was secure — and besides, they had speeches to write and shoes to buy. The big end-of-the-year report on India got short shrift until the weekend before it was due. By Sunday night, having done nothing for two days but work on it, Sarah was mad at herself for putting it off, mad at the report for impinging on her weekend plans, and mad at me because I was a convenient target.

"You should have reminded me," she said, even though she was already on record as hating to be nagged.

My wicked, petulant, inner voice replied, No, I shouldn't have. The principal told us to let you make your own mistakes. Too bad for you. So there.

She continued to complain about how I had ruined her life. I worked the Sunday crossword puzzle and spun the dial on my internal radio station. Ah. There was Lyn Brown again, chanting the mantra of the well-mannered mother:

"'I hate you' is the most important part of the connection. . . . It's an incredible compliment to a mother, even though it feels terrible."

I should have been flattered when Sarah said I'd let her down and thrilled to hear that she thought this was a stupid assignment from a teacher she no longer liked — clearly part of a larger plot to keep her from enjoying a kid's life. Didn't the adults in her universe remember that she was only eleven years old? Wouldn't she have the opportunity to be overworked when she was older?

Lyn Brown said, "The onus is on the mother to be an adult."

Yeah, well, nobody's perfect.

"Look, Daddy and I are responsible for paying for a wonderful school for you, which is what we wanted to do," I said, even though I had recently horrified myself by totaling up what that wonderful education would cost by the time she collected her college diploma. "That's our side of the bargain. Your side of the bargain is to be responsible and do your best."

I could have, I should have, left it at that, but she was giving me the same kind of condescending stare I had given the rabbi when he asked who still didn't believe in God. I had become the dread, droning voice of authority, and she had tuned me out. I upped the ante.

"If you are not going to take this seriously," I said, appalled at what I knew I was about to say, "then Daddy and I are not going to keep working this hard to send you to school. It is a privilege. You don't just get to do it."

She stormed out of the room, leaving me alone with the hideousness of me. Puzzle books still included that game where there were ten things wrong with a seemingly reasonable picture: a man with a shoe on his head, or a goldfish with a cat's face. How many things were wrong with me? I had issued a threat I had no intention of executing, I had guilt-tripped, I had insulted her by implying that she had made a conscious decision to mess up. I had taken her literally instead of addressing her frustration. I had, in short, been a brat instead of a mother, and I had given her cause to fire me, if only temporarily.

Worst of all, I had seen it coming, and I had not been able to stop myself. In the waning days of my administration, I had pulled out the stops, just to show that I still could.

APOLOGY, THESE DAYS, is a cheap, offhand thrill; we can act as badly as we like, as long as we say we are sorry afterward. A guy in a hot car cut me off to get into the parking space I was waiting for, but he wasn't about to relinquish it, not even when I pulled up right next to him and gave him my best steely glare. His pantomimed "sorry" was his ticket into heaven. People elbowed past the line at the farmers' market, paid for their stuff ahead of the rest of us, and shrugged and said "sorry" as they walked away. I left my shoes all over the house, apologized, and forgot to put them away next time, and Larry had the same relationship with the crumbs he never brushed off the kitchen counter.

I suppose it is some kind of progress at least to acknowledge our shortcomings. My parents never apologized to my sister and me, because to apologize was to cede authority, or the illusion of authority. My father said incredibly rude things about my motoring ability when I tried to drive home my brand-new college graduation present, which had a stick shift, but he never would have thought to apologize, because parents were more powerful than their children, and so, beyond rebuke.

I liked the idea of contrition, the soul's equivalent of an exfoliating facial scrub. I just wasn't very good at it, at least not yet. Rosalind Wiseman, the author of *Queen Bees and Wannabes,* has worked with teens to avert violence since 1994, when she cofounded the Empowerment Program in Washington, D.C., and the art of the sincere apology is one of the fundamentals of her approach, whether it is between girls and girls, girls and boys, boys and boys, or teens and their parents. She told me her formula: "There has to be an understanding of the crime committed, on the part of the apologizer, and it can't involve any back-and-forth, any 'And you did this,'" she said. "It's genuinely contrite, no last licks, and it comes without the expectation of a returned apology. It means you genuinely respect the other person's humanity, their right to exist on the planet. Teaching kids to apologize is one of the big responsibilities a parent has. They should see us doing it."

I told Sarah I was sorry for having issued a meaningless ultimatum and for bringing up how much school cost, which had nothing to do with anything. I told her I was sorry for being a remorse klutz, but I was sure I would have ample opportunity in the future to hone my apology skills.

THERE WAS A TIME, not all that long ago, when I still had standards. I did not sing in public, I never purposely owned an outfit that matched someone else's, save for that brief interlude when Sarah and I had identical overalls and striped T-shirts, and I never, ever got involved in any parenting activity that I would be embarrassed to confess to my childless pals. That was before Phyllis and I offered to cochair the end-of-the-year teacher appreciation luncheon at school. Work had kept us from the ongoing volunteer efforts, like serving hot lunch or helping out in the library, but we intended to go out in a blaze of helpful glory.

That was how I ended up in a chorus line of a dozen moms, each of us wearing black slacks and a souvenir California T-shirt, doing as high a cancan kick as creaky joints would allow, as we sang a song about our school to the tune of the Beach Boys' "California Girls." Sarah and Julia were inordinately proud, and thank goodness, no one thought to bring a video camera.

That same day, while we were serving the goat cheese salad and the marinated chicken, Larry got a phone call from a company that wanted him to work on a project for an automotive client. Lots of work. Six weeks of it, to be exact, on the corporate pay scale that had been our salvation of late. It was the perfect job — except that it overlapped the three weeks when we were supposed to be in Italy together.

We were two weeks from graduation, and we were supposed to leave two days after that. He did not say no immediately, which impressed and terrified me.

"If I were thirty, I'd say no," he said. "But we've got a kid in private school, the economy's a mess, and I just don't see how I can turn it down."

WHAT REALLY SEPARATES parents from the childless is what an overworked friend delicately calls the "fuck-you factor" — the ability to turn away from responsibility because you feel like it.

People in their twenties have a high FU factor because they have all the time in the world to make up for their mistakes, and because the only mouths they have to feed are their own. People without children have it, unless they are enslaved by their own expensive tastes. We used to have it. We no longer do.

Larry thought about the job overnight, and the next morning he said, "You guys go."

I said I would cancel the whole trip, which turned out to be the only thing dumber than going without him. We did not have trip insurance, and we had rented a house and then a little apartment, because it sounded like more fun, and less expense, than a hotel. We were too close to the travel date to get any of our money back, so the choices were bad and worse: Sarah and I could go without him, or we could all stay home and watch well over a thousand dollars fly right out the window.

Harry and Judith were supposed to spend the first week with us, and they'd be fine on their own; they traveled all over the world. But Hummie and Vicky and their two girls, our Seattle friends, planned to join us for weeks two and three, and that was because — drum roll, please — it was their first family trip to Italy. They had said for years that they wanted to make their inaugural overseas trip with us.

There was no good solution.

"Just go," Larry said. "You'll have a whole month with Sarah. It'll be one of those mother-daughter things you never forget. The trip of a lifetime."

One of those things you never forget — not necessarily a happy thought. I almost lost my two front teeth in a car crash with my father when I was eight. My sister and I had sequential German measles. A boy stood me up for a date and everyone at my high school knew it. I picked the wrong college and had to transfer as a sophomore. I picked the wrong guy more than once. I remember all of those things.

I loved the idea of a long Italian adventure with Sarah, and I quaked at the very thought of it. This could be our chance to cement the bond between us — our week together, times four. Or this could be a disaster, a long enough one to ensure that she never, ever forgot it.

For starters, I would be completely responsible for getting around, in a country where Larry had intended to do all the driving. He suggested that I cancel the rental car and travel by train instead, and I had an early glimpse of how tricky things could get. I could dodge Ferraris on the autostrada, where even stalled cars seemed to move at eighty miles an hour, or I could roust Sarah from bed to dash to the train station for the single connecting train to our next city.

With the car, the challenge was mine; with the train, the challenge was getting Sarah to do things she might not want to do. I kept the car. I called our fellow travelers with the bad news, and late at night I chanted private little voodoo chants in the faint hope that the automotive client would fire the company that had hired Larry, even though that was not a very grown-up thing to want.

17 Graduation

OUR SCHOOL TOOK THE LAMAZE APPROACH TO GRADUAtion: Keep the mothers so busy huffing and puffing that they do not notice the pain of separation. Like labor, the days that led up to the great event involved wild anticipation and the rueful sense that this kind of fun was going to involve moments of regret, however fleeting. The mothers who had preceded us had established traditions to celebrate the departing sixth graders — a class trip to Universal City Walk, an afternoon of photos in a nearby park, the pajama breakfast. The planning and execution of those events, like the Lamaze breathing patterns, kept the moms from falling apart.

The front-row moms were the core of the organizational team — Lori because she had done it for her older daughter, and Phyllis, Jo Ann, and I because three diligent working women were ready to play a little hooky. Two weeks before graduation, we convened at another mother's office for a final meeting. Lori had photographs from every one of the sixth-grade events so far, with prints for each kid in each picture, and it was up to us to make thirty-six customized photo albums. Sarah would be in every picture in her album, as Julia and Aviva and Emily would be in every picture in theirs. It was a perfect mix of narcissism and nostalgia.

What we had, when we were done, were little flip books of life; riffle the pages and watch sixth grade fly by.

We drew up a car-pool list for the pajama breakfast, and we filled little white gift bags with graduation memorabilia, including big white T-shirts with photos on the back of everyone in the class. We discussed the girls' graduation dresses in microscopic detail, and we consoled each other over not having heard a single syllable of a graduation speech.

We were at the fulcrum of the school phase of life — seven years of school gone, six years left before college. More than halfway there — much more, if we counted preschool, which we chose not to do. We were more than halfway through a friendship that revolved around our children, and I wondered about the centrifugal force of this life. We had gotten lucky, with all the girls going to the same school next year, but what would happen when they spun further out, to college?

We had not come into this with the same plan. Lori and Roy dreamed of retiring near a golf course in Palm Springs, and sometimes Phyllis speculated that she and Raphe might head out of town, once their two girls were in college. I couldn't imagine Jo Ann and Jay anywhere but Los Angeles — but then, there was a time when I couldn't imagine having a child, so who's to say. I often said that I would move east in a minute if we could figure out what to do once we got there, but I was not sure I meant it; a new fence and some shrubs might be enough change of scene for me.

Once the girls moved on, I expected that all of us would, too, our friendship reduced to e-mails and holiday cards and the occasional drop-by on the way to someplace else. It was an odd thought, and distant, and I chose to dismiss it, as Phyllis chose to dismiss whatever meeting she should have left for instead of sticking around for another pot of coffee. We consulted our watches, and we lingered, regardless.

THERE WAS A STRANGE and enduring tradition at Sarah's school that involved grabbing the sixth graders out of their beds at dawn and taking them out to breakfast, still in their pajamas, before they went to school. The principal had fibbed this year and said that breakfast was canceled, in an attempt to restore an element of surprise, but apparently nobody fell for it. Too much of the sleepwear still had its store creases.

The banquet room at the local Denny's was set up with three long tables, and the parent chauffeurs, myself included, were exiled to an adjacent dining room. The first kids to arrive immediately staked out two of the tables, one for the boys, one for the girls. When the next group arrived, it all came undone. The cool girls took over the third table. One of them slung her arm over the back of an empty chair and beckoned to a particular friend — and just like that, the new table was the better table, seats by invitation only. A couple of girls jumped up as soon as their names were called. A couple of girls whose names were not called jumped up anyhow and muscled their way into the preferred seating.

One girl saved a seat for Sarah. Julia, who was already on her feet, said, "C'mon," but Sarah did not budge. Another girl took the coveted chair, and Sarah was left behind with the uninvited. I could see that she was unhappy, but she did not move. The leftovers moved to fill in the vacancies at her table, and Sarah sat at the head, trying to chat. She glanced at me once through the window.

The chosen people, over at the first table, were just as animated as you might expect. Sarah's table looked more like the board meeting of a dying dot-com.

On the way back to the cars after breakfast, she leaned into me and confessed that she didn't have a very good time.

"I wasn't sitting with who I wanted to sit with," she said.

"I could see that," I said, fighting the urge to talk about the sterling qualities of some of her tablemates. "I noticed when the girls called you over, you didn't get up."

I sounded like tepid milk tastes, and Sarah resented it. "I couldn't, Mom. The other girls were going to feel so bad for being left out. Nobody was calling their names. But it wasn't any fun. I don't get what the point of the breakfast was. I could've slept later."

"Well, I admire what you did," I said. "Next time there's a class event, I think you can let yourself do what you want. But you were a loyal friend, and I was proud of you." Now that was useful advice: Do what you want, but please continue to be compassionate to the girls at the unpopular table. Sarah was not a contortionist, and yet I expected her to be in two places at once.

My father used to dismiss all worthless platitudes with a single response: "That and a quarter," he would say, "will get you a cup of coffee."

I heard his dry tone in Sarah's voice. "Next time," she said, "I'm going to sit with whoever I want to sit with."

I doubted it. Members of the popular clique needed to reject other girls to feel superior, and Sarah now had firsthand experience of how it felt to be on the outside. Every time she got invited to join the other table, she'd likely remember this morning. She could react by hardening her heart and grabbing a chair, fast, but I looked at her worn expression and guessed that she would not. Next time it would be even more difficult to make that move.

THE PUBLIC SARAH was ready to graduate. Gary had finished her coat and dress, and she found a pair of shoes that had heels but not Heels. She listened to all the chat about hairdos and brushed her hair this way and that. She auditioned various barrettes. She rehearsed her speech.

The private Sarah knew that her life so far was about to become past tense, so she tried to slow things down. Psychologists call it regression: Toddlers get to preschool and forget their toilet training, kids go to kindergarten or summer camp and cry for the same parents they had taken for granted the day before. Sixth graders get ready to become the youngest students at a new school, and the weight of that makes them yearn for the good old days, when they could lord it over the little kids.

One night, right before bed, she climbed into our bed and nestled against me.

"I'll always be your baby," she said, out of nowhere. "And you'll always be thirty-nine, almost forty years older than I am."

"Always. We march into the future."

She was quiet for a moment.

"So when I'm sixty," she said, "you'll be almost one hundred."

"There's a thought," I replied. Grandma Ethel did live to be almost 102.

Sarah must have had the same thought.

"I won't let you live in a nursing home like Great-Grandma Ethel," she said. "You and Daddy can come and live with me." No matter that Larry would by then be closing in on 109; this was the heart, not the head, talking.

She imagined that a lifetime from now, we might still hang out together. I was proud, I was touched — and at the same time, I wondered if we had inadvertently failed to raise a new woman. The first female president of the United States was probably not going to be the kind of gal who longed for the days when she was mommy's baby, and if a woman discovered the cure for cancer, it was likely not going to be because she was kind to her elderly relatives. There were attributes traditionally considered to be male and attributes traditionally considered to be female, and without realizing it, we might have loaded Sarah up with old-fashioned virtues.

Some of the critics who took Carol Gilligan and Lyn Brown to task in the early 1990s were disturbed by what they saw as a latent sexism lurking in the two researchers' theories about adolescent girls. They acknowledged the fact that models of "healthy" emotional behavior were based on men's lives, just as most medical research focused on men's ailments, and that the authors were looking for new definitions that were appropriate for teenage girls. Still, they feared that Gilligan and Brown had unwittingly reinforced the stereotype of the nice, nurturing female by writing about girls who spoke with a "care voice," a secondary, moral voice, unlike the more highly evolved "justice voice" that men tended to use.

Dr. Linda Kerber, a University of Iowa history professor who has written extensively on gender, authority, and the law, told the *New York Times Magazine* that she was particularly concerned about descriptions that recalled the "romantic sentimentalism of old voices in the women's movement, with their notions of women as more peaceable than men." She accused Gilligan and Brown of ignoring issues of economics, race, and gender politics and insisted that the real issue was social, not psychological.

At the time, Gilligan had replied, "'Care' isn't simply a matter of being 'the nice girl' or 'the perfect woman' — it's about being responsible to oneself as well as to others." Eleven years later, in the midst of international conflicts and economic woes, it seemed to me that the old justice voice might not be all it was cracked up to be and that things could not have been worse if we'd listened a bit more to the care voice — might have been better, for that matter. Perhaps it was time to revisit the national hierarchy of voices, which, after all, had been determined by men in the first place.

SARAH AND I were not really talking about my living with her when she was my age. She just wanted to make it plain that Larry and I mattered, wherever we ended up when we were ancient.

"Thank you," I said. "That's very kind. I will try to be a good guest and not get in the way. I could read to your kids."

"Okay," she said, and trundled off to bed.

THERE I WAS, a middle-aged writer with no music chops left at all, playing air guitar on a stranger's front lawn. Larry watched my fingers wriggle, as he had on the ride over here, and he stepped close to whisper, "How'd you get into this?"

"She asked me," I replied, and I picked up my guitar case and went inside.

It was time for Sarah's annual piano recital, but this year was different for two reasons: My mom was in town, and I had agreed to play a duet with Sarah, she on the piano, I on one of the two guitars I still kept in the closet. I had calluses on the fingers of my left hand for the first time in twenty-five years, and I was scared that I would not remember the chord progression for the song Sarah had chosen, the world's simplest arrangement of the Beatles' "I'll Follow the Sun."

We took our seats on white folding chairs in our hosts' living room, and the piano teacher made her annual speech about the great achievement of simply playing in front of strangers. It was a benevolent crowd. We applauded for the first little girl, who flubbed her piece right off the bat. We went wild for the dad of the house, who could not get through a duet with his son and apologized with a big kiss on the boy's forehead. When it was the dad's turn for a solo, he abandoned the piece he had meant to play so that they could have another go at the duet. From where I sat, I could see his fingers tremble as he searched for the right notes and failed to find them. He blew it again. The applause only got louder.

When it was our turn, I muttered to Sarah, "Play slow enough so that I can keep up with you."

And then I went into a trance. I sat just behind her and to one side, and when she put her hands on the keyboard, my brain went dead. Only my fingers still worked, left hand marching up and down the neck of the guitar, right hand strumming with what sounded like the right beat. Somehow we got to the end of the piece, without any conscious help from me, thanks, and when we were done Sarah gave me such a smile that I thought I would faint.

For eleven years I had tried to be an admirable role model for a modern daughter: I juggled career and family, I was a more-than-decent cook, I made our home a place where her friends and our extended family felt welcome. I tried to argue with Larry only about important things, and I failed, but at least she saw the effort. I read and considered and debated with him about how best to raise a girl, since we had far more desire than expertise. I replayed conversations, thought of what I might have said better, and then said it, even though Sarah had long since forgotten the original exchange.

For all that, I had gotten to today without understanding what I was really after. It was this: To take a flyer, every now and then. To be drawn outside the lines that defined our daily life, however briefly, and to be open to surprise. Someday Sarah's life with us would be condensed into a paraphrase. She would select stories that characterized her childhood, and those would be what she took with her into her adult life, just as we had selected souvenirs from elementary school and packed them up in a box, leaving the insignificant details to be slowly forgotten. She would explain who she was with anecdotes, since there was no way to remember, let alone tell, the whole story. I wanted her to recall that we had done things we might never have done — like playing music together in front of an audience — if love, if family, had not pulled us somewhere new.

As I walked past my mother, I heard her tell a stranger that I had been a very talented little musician as a child and that I had taught guitar, briefly, as an adult — this from a woman who warned me, in the weeks after my father's death, that she was not a "huggy, kissy person like he was," and I had best not expect a lot of demonstrable affection in his absence. And yet, there she was bragging. She was proud to be my mom.

I felt bold enough to approach the woman whose house it was, even though I didn't know her, to say how wonderful her husband and stepson had been and how I admired her husband's decision to try the duet a second time. I said I imagined that the duet would be one of those family stories that got told over and over again.

"No," she said. "The important thing is that his son will carry it in his heart. And you and your daughter will carry this day forever." I was a little frightened by her intensity, but she wouldn't let me go.

"I cried," she said. "I cried when you and your daughter played."

* * *

THE NIGHT BEFORE graduation, Sarah asked me, "Mom, have you decided how you're wearing your hair to graduation yet?"

"No. Why?" I never thought about how to wear my hair, unless "out of the way" constituted a hairstyle. I kept it clean and out of my eyes, and it was nice, forgiving hair, and that had always been that.

"Well, if I wear mine with the front pulled back, would you wear yours a different way?"

I had worn my hair that way for most of my adult life.

"Sure," I said.

THE SIXTH-GRADE GRADUATION processional was a big deal at our school. The graduates submitted three photographs — one from when they were little, one current portrait, and one with their pals — that were projected onto a screen as each student entered the auditorium, this year to the heart-wrenching strains of Sara McLaughlin singing "I Will Remember You." The whole thing was calculated for maximum effect, and it never failed. By the end of the processional, the audience was one big teary swamp.

We had picked a photo of a tousled four-year-old Sarah in a flannel nightgown, sitting on a little wooden chair with an ankle resting on the other knee, a very large book balanced on her leg. It got a collective *aaah* of recognition, for that was how people thought of her: a serious girl with an enigmatic grin, lost in her head, happy. I stared at it as a young woman in a pretty coat, the new Sarah, strode past and took her seat onstage.

Each child had a minute to speak, and we would have known who was who even if the principal had read all the speeches for them. Emily was all inside jokes and antics, and she may have been the first graduate to use the word *boogers* in a speech. Sarah reminisced about kindergarten and wondered how she had so quickly become one of the big kids she used to idolize. Julia's speech was full of gratitude to her family. Aviva tried to get through sixty seconds on friendship, but one of her friends, a girl she had known since preschool, was going to a different school for seventh grade, and Aviva started to cry as soon as she mentioned the girl's name.

From there, it got worse — she gasped for breath, she could not go on, she had to go on, and Jo Ann sat next to me the way I had sat still while Sarah adjusted her stirrups. The way I now sat still when she went over a two-foot jump, and fell off with a thud, and got back on again. It was our job to sit still, even as it was our instinct to rush forward. We smiled at Aviva with great force of will, the whole row of front-row moms and dads, and somehow she got to the end of her minute.

TWO DAYS LATER, Sarah and I had started down the jetway to board our plane when I balked and backed up to get one more glimpse of Larry, who remained rooted to the spot as though he knew I would reappear. Of course he did. In sixteen years of marriage, we had never been separated for more than a single week. A month apart was a hell of a way to be reminded that we preferred to be together.

We waved and blew kisses, and then Sarah and I proceeded to the plane so that we could fly halfway around the world. I reminded myself that this was a great opportunity for us to spend some time together; we'd be solid when she hit seventh grade, ready for the big time. We had the summer to prepare for the unknown, just as we had prepared for the mystery of this month abroad — except the more I thought about it, the less prepared I felt.

I had a folder full of paperwork, plane tickets, the car reservation form, hotel confirmations at each end of the trip, rental confirmations in between, an itinerary, and pages and pages of driving directions. I had an international cell phone and two guidebooks. I knew exactly where we would be on any given day, but I had not a clue as to what we would be doing. By the time the airplane icon on the airline map had blipped its way across the continent and headed out over the Atlantic Ocean, I had traded bravado for uncertainty. How could wc possibly prepare for Europe, for adolescence, for anything? We had no real idea of what was coming—only that its arrival was imminent.

18 Riding on Pasta

THE RENTAL CAR WOULDN'T MOVE — OR RATHER, IT wouldn't move backward. Forward was easy: After a jet-lagged early dinner and a good night's sleep, Sarah and I took a cab to the car rental office in Milan, picked up a little sedan and a map, and drove back to the hotel to get our luggage, along the exact route the cab had taken. We were in sight of our destination, three blocks, tops, when we realized that the last few streets were one way in the wrong direction. I pulled over to consult the map, and then I shifted into reverse to get out of the parking space.

We moved forward — not a good thing, since there were maybe twelve inches between me and the car in front of me. Now there were nine. After another attempt, six.

"Put it in reverse," said Sarah, with an urgent, anxious note in her voice. It was Sunday morning, which meant that most of Milan was in church. I was all that stood between Sarah and being stranded in a large foreign city, and right now I was not behaving in a reassuring way.

"I am trying," I said, grinding both my teeth and the clutch. I was furious at myself for having forgotten the fundamental law of car rental: Try out everything before you leave the lot. My next attempt was my last. I could not fit a strand of fettucine between my bumper and the car in front of me.

I fought the urge to abandon the car, walk back to the hotel, and head for the airport. My rage was complicated: I hated my own incompetence, Sarah's abject dependence, Larry's mature decision to stay behind, even my lack of patriotism. If I had settled for a stateside trip, with an American car and English-speaking natives, we would not be in such desperate straits. I had let my child down, in a place where she already felt insecure, and the more I stared at the dashboard, the angrier I became. I had embraced the idea that this trip was an unexpected chance to build a cache of memories that would sustain us through the coming years. So far, all I had given Sarah was a wicked anecdote about how her mom ended the vacation before it began.

I opened and shut the empty glove box. Language skills were only valuable if there was an owner's manual to read.

"You would think that they would give you the information you need to drive the goddamned, excuse me, car," I grumbled. I gave the steering wheel a couple of good whacks with my palm. "I cannot believe that we are sitting here, unable to move."

Sarah cowered at the far edge of her seat.

"Don't look at me like that. I am doing the best I can, and we will get out of here."

"I'm not looking at you," she squealed, fighting tears.

"This is great," I muttered. "This is going to be a wonderful vacation."

There it was: car trouble to the apocalypse, in thirty seconds flat. In addition to everything else, now I could hate myself for snapping at Sarah, for having forgotten how to drive a stick shift, for making her feel anxious, for starting our vacation on the wrong foot, for setting a tone that would no doubt poison the rest of our vacation time together. Less than a day into our escapade, I had failed not only Sarah but myself. I had behaved as though sarcasm were a communications tool.

I had to get out of the parking spot. I took a cleansing breath, shook out the fingers on my right hand, and grasped the stick shift for what would have to be the last time.

This time I felt the little ring that sits under the head of the gear shift on European cars, the one I had forgotten about, the one I had to pull up, as I shifted, to get the car into reverse. The car slid back, as silky as a couture model on a Milan catwalk. So what if we drove in circles three times, searching in vain for a street that went the way I wanted to go? At least we were moving. I spied a cabbie waiting for a nonexistent fare, summoned up all of my Italian, and asked him please to drive very slowly to the Hotel Spadari so that we could follow him. I would pay him the regular fare.

He guided us back. We loaded our bags and some groceries into the trunk and followed the wonderfully large, clear signs on the dependably two-way streets that led to the autostrada, heading south.

WITH A SLEEPY TRAVELING COMPANION and four hours of driving ahead of me, I had all the time in the world to berate myself. I was as bad as that new breed of mother I disdained — the ones who condemned their lives wholesale because they had had one too many sleepless nights, the ones who regarded parenting as largely an inconvenience they wished they could reconsider. Perhaps it was a consequence of their lives' having been too easy until now, but their hostility was palpable, and as Sarah's principal often said, children know everything, even if you think they don't hear you, even if they don't yet have the words to express what they know.

These women offended me mightily. They were not unlike the martyr moms of my mother's generation, except that the first martyrs didn't realize what had happened to them until the kids were grown and gone. The second martyrs, the new ones, came to motherhood with their own high-end consumer profiles and social lives and Pilates abs, all of them temporarily sacrificed on a pyre of preschool applications. They knew exactly what they were missing, and they wanted the world to know that they had been robbed.

They had lost the long view, and in my first twenty-four hours in Italy, I had been no better. There was no erasing it, but when we got off the autostrada for a cold drink, I told Sarah that I was sorry I had gotten so frazzled.

She shrugged, so I upped the ante. I told her she had a free pass to get angry and sarcastic and expect complete understanding in return, at least once.

WE SPENT OUR FIRST WEEK with her godparents, Harry and Judith, at a house tucked so far into an Umbrian hillside that we had to slow down and turn on the car's bright lights, even when the route became familiar, to make sure we did not miss the turnoff. We ate and walked and looked at churches, both sacred and retail, and then they were gone, replaced by our Seattle friends, Vicky and Hummie, and their two daughters — Jessi, who was Sarah's age, and their Sarah, who was three years older.

Sarah and I drove all the way down to the gas station by the autostrada exit to escort them up the winding road to the house, and the minute we saw them, everything changed. Sarah had siblings, and for the next two weeks she did not need me to be her constant companion. When her godparents were there, I was as close as she was going to get to a peer. She could count on me to stay home and eat pasta with her if she didn't want a big, drawn-out meal, and when she hit the wall, churchwise, I ducked out with her to look at ancient typewriters at a nearby flea market. She preferred sharing a room with me to having one all to herself, and we did not have a single quarrel.

Now the numbers were even — three adults, three girls, and no need to cross party lines. That first night, Sarah moved out of the room we'd been sharing and set up camp downstairs with the other girls. Then they set out to show us just how influential peers can be. The sisters encouraged Sarah to announce that she did not need to see the inside of one more church. The three girls could not be budged in the morning until their hair had been braided properly. If one of them had to have lunch, the other two got hungry, and even though all six of us sat at the same table in a restaurant, the conversation rarely crossed generations.

ONE AFTERNOON, TOWARD THE END of our stay in Umbria, we went to Perugia, famed for its *passagiata,* the stroll before dinner. We were at an outdoor table in the middle of the broad main promenade when the clock struck six. Suddenly people poured out of doorways and began to walk the long loop from the church, at one end, to the little park at the other. Hundreds of people passed by us — two diminutive ladies in dark clothes and head scarves, a tall woman in spandex on the arm of a short man in white, a phalanx of girls in summer dresses, and behind them, a willing bunch of boys looking for romance. We picked out our favorites and made up stories about them. We lingered past sunset.

When we were ready to leave, we went inside the café to buy desserts to take home, but the cashier warned me not to go home, not yet. There was music in the square tonight, singing clubs from all over the region, she said, and we should not miss it.

Sure enough, there were three hundred people standing on the steps of the church, framed by big standing speakers and stage lights. Their first song was something about love and tears, and it must have been a local favorite, because everyone else in the crowd went all soft when they heard it. No one seemed to care that the singers were slightly out of tune and out of sync, the northern end of the group a beat ahead of the southern end. Couples put their arms around each other, and parents stopped shushing the kids long enough to steal a kiss.

I stared at the moon and wondered how I had ever gotten so lucky, to be here on this particular night. The singers all looked like they were in their seventies or eighties. They might have grown children who long ago had emigrated to the United States, or who lived here still and snickered, privately, at the glee club's efforts. Some of them might never have had children, which was why they had so much time to sing. It was beside the point. All that mattered was that they had traveled here, in groups of ten and twenty, dressed up, to assemble under the stars, just as they had last year, just as they would next year.

I grabbed Sarah around her shoulders and held her tight. I kissed the top of her head and whispered, "I love this." I had a friend, a long time ago, who married a much older man, and he warned her that she needed to prepare for two new lives — the one they would have together, and the quite possibly longer one she would have after he died. He wasn't being maudlin. He simply wanted her to give that second life its due.

I said to myself, Please, when I am eighty, let me stand in a square with my friends and sing.

I HAD ARRANGED for an afternoon of horseback riding for Sarah and me, since the other girls' combined experience amounted to two trail rides and a couple of lessons. I had not taken the peer factor into account. They desperately wanted to go with us, and Vicky said she would come, too.

We started out across a field of wheat, accompanied by the husband of the woman who had set up the ride, and by two younger kids who rode regularly. "We ride now across next year's pasta," our guide proclaimed, and I figured we were in for a fairly magical time, the wheat tickling the horses' bellies, a lake in the far distance, wildflowers everywhere.

Then the older Sarah's pony spooked at a plastic bag hanging on a fence post, and she went flying. I yelled a word of caution and a bit of fast advice about how best to take a fall. When my Sarah's horse bolted, as part of the plastic bag chain reaction, I called to her to hang on. Any parent who has ever witnessed a threat to her child's safety knows that these reactions are involuntary. In this case, they were unwelcome as well.

We were riding down a narrow trail, under a thicket of trees, when I caught up to my Sarah, who turned around and fairly spat at me.

"You," she seethed, "are not helping at all." Then she turned away and kicked her horse, just enough to move him away from me.

How cruel was that? Tears made rivulets of mud in the dust on my face as I tried to figure out exactly what crime I had committed. Clearly, I should have kept my mouth shut when the Sarahs fell off and threatened to fall off, respectively, because then I could not be accused of not helping. That sounded backward: By trying to help, I had not helped, no, I had made matters much worse, so bad, in fact, that my child had felt the need to snarl at me in the midst of paradise.

There is no room for self-pity on a horse, so I focused on forward motion and said nothing until we had to cross a small, rocky irrigation trough. Actually, I didn't say anything then, either, but Sarah accused me of having moaned, clear proof of my worrywart tendencies.

I explained that it was a happy noise, not a fearful one, that I had exclaimed at the silvery bits of thistle flower that floated through the air.

"I was happy," I said. "It had nothing to do with crossing this ditch. And I cannot let you talk to me in that tone of voice."

"It's because you've been yelling at me all morning," she replied.

"I have not."

"You've been yelling at me all morning," she insisted, "like you're yelling at me now."

"I am not yelling." It struck me that we had entered the land of "are too, am not," which is the verbal equivalent of quicksand. I understood that she was secretly anxious — a strange horse, the great out-of-doors, a guide who spoke less English than I did Italian, and waves of fear rising from the other Sarah. I understood that she resented me for knowing her secret, but I was wearing a flimsy helmet on a tall horse, and I was not inclined to be her punching bag.

"I am furious at the way you are behaving, and you have hurt my feelings," I said, and I pointed my horse at the irrigation ditch.

Wow. No maneuvers, no psychodrama, just, You made me feel bad and right now I don't like you. Honest, if clumsy — and as it turned out, effective. Once everyone was safely across the ditch, Sarah turned to me, with that beguiling smile of hers, and pointed out the lavender flowers that blanketed the field.

"Look, Mommy," she said. "We could just lean over and get some of these to press."

"Yes, we could," I agreed, and that was that. Everyone got to behave badly once in a while, and then we got to leave it behind.

THAT NIGHT SARAH CAME UPSTAIRS after all of us had gone to bed and crawled into bed next to me.

"This turned out to be a very nice day," I said.

"I had a wonderful time on the horse," she said.

"I could see that. You even got to trot."

"A little."

"And lead the way."

"I know."

She gave me a kiss and a hug, leaped up from the bed, and headed down the hall at a canter. I could hear the waltz time of her steps, *one* two three, *one* two three — and then, as she rounded the corner toward the stairs, I heard the jubilant cry of a girl who knew that it was the horse's right leg forward first, going clockwise, and left leg forward first, going counterclockwise:

"I'm on the right lead!"

BY THE TIME we all headed up to Florence a week later, the girls agreed among themselves on everything — that it was a good idea to eat gelato at ten o'clock in the morning, that it was too hot for the science museum, that an hour at the Uffizi was plenty.

They giggled and joked and played cards, they stormed to the top of a church tower in a downpour, and at night they all gathered in one apartment until bedtime. I watched and wondered if this was what seventh grade would be like, if Sarah would peel away as easily as this. I wasn't sad. It was nice to walk around with Vicky and catch up, since neither of us was very good at the prolonged phone chat. I looked forward to a morning espresso with Hummie at the little bar across the street from our apartments.

Whom was I kidding? Of course I wasn't sad; I knew I was going to get Sarah back again in a matter of days. I could revel in my newfound autonomy — and hers — because it couldn't last.

WE STOOD ON THE STEPS of the church in Siena, stumped. The adults had been very accommodating about the girls' desire to cut back on churches, but we had taken the train all the way here to see this one. So far we had not gotten past the door. A security guard stood in our way, pointed at a big multilingual sign, and then at the older Sarah. We retreated down the steps.

Italian churches prohibit women from entering in sleeveless tops or very short shorts, and Sarah qualified on both counts, since she was wearing a tank top and gym shorts turned over at the waistband. Years back, when breasts were merely a theoretical concept, Vicky and Hummie had staked out their position: absolutely, positively no tank tops. No daughter of theirs was going to parade around like that.

And yet here we were, frying in the midday sun while more than a few secular citizens — young male ones — cast approving glances in the older Sarah's direction. In desperation, we bought a souvenir regional flag and made a cape for Sarah's shoulders, turned an extra shirt into a wraparound skirt, and marched into the church. But I did wonder what had happened to Vicky and Hummie's wardrobe restrictions.

Vicky shrugged. Her daughters' friends all wore tank tops, and at some point being a weirdo seemed a bigger problem than being underdressed. Good parents were flexible. They had to trust that they had raised Sarah not to live up to the packaging, and besides, it was so ridiculously hot.

ON OUR LAST NIGHT in Florence, I bullied everyone into walking back to the Piazza Signoria to say good-bye to the square. We stood around, we listened to a violinist, and at 9:00 we headed off for our evening gelato. The stars were not yet out, but the sky was a crazy dark blue, not daytime blue, not nighttime. Vicky and I agreed that there was no point in taking a photograph because the color would never come out right.

I asked Sarah what she would call it.

"True blue," she said.

The next morning we set off on our week alone. We walked for three hours between one little coastal town and the next, we read in bed every night, we strolled arm in arm and watched the world go by, and we ate fish we never saw at home. One morning in Venice, emboldened, Sarah wandered around the Piazza San Marco while I finished my coffee and a book. I looked up and she was gone, only to reappear a moment later, gone again, and back. I put the book down and watched her wander, looking in a store window or down a side street, and suddenly I could imagine her here someday without me — or Larry and me having coffee on this very spot without her.

We called him from everywhere, and toward the end we felt a tug. It was time to go home.

I had flirted with alienation on this trip. I had ventured down the path that led to the generally expected outcome with a daughter, only to be drawn back to Sarah by the singers in the square and the night sky, and by smaller things that I had tucked into a notebook to keep for myself, along with the lavender flowers that were almost dry.

Whoever wrote this part of the story threw in a Greek chorus of traveling mothers for good measure, women who struck up conversations with us in train stations, in restaurants, or sitting in a hotel lobby late at night — women who turned out, all of them, to be mothers of older girls. They appeared out of the wings, spoke their lines, and just as quickly vanished. Each time they said the exact same thing: We took a trip like yours once, and we will never forget it.

19 Letting Go

THE CURRICULUM GUIDE FOR SARAH'S NEW SCHOOL READ like a great menu; it was hard to imagine wanting anything that wasn't already there. The incoming seventh graders had no choice about which classes they took, but I leafed through the booklet anyhow and thought about what she might like to take in the coming years. I allowed myself to pick a few classes that appealed to me, too.

For an instant, I envied her. Parents proudly talked about giving their children more opportunities than they had had, and my family was no exception: Neither of my grandmothers, and only one of my grandfathers, had gone to college; my dad got his bachelor's degree, but my mom's family could only afford a two-year school. I knew, from the minute I could tally my birthday savings bonds, that my entire family intended for me to go not just to college but to graduate school, if I wanted to. And yet they never said how it felt to have a child who had more choices in life than they had.

We wanted Sarah to explore worlds that were long since closed to us, if she so chose — chemistry or art history, math or metalworking, they were all in the catalog. She could learn things that didn't even exist in my high school curriculum, like digital animation. Her life was full of choice; ours, in varying permutations, was all about words on paper.

I wondered what we would talk about if she sailed off in a direction that was utterly foreign to us. We had no friends who were chemists, because it was hard to have a close relationship with someone who spoke a completely different dialect. That was the chance we were taking. We wanted to give her a larger world than ours, knowing that we would have less in common because of it. We traded the hothouse intimacy of her early life for the vast unknown, and we vowed to keep our small misgivings — whether about chemistry or about that hypothetical beau imported from outside our frame of reference — to ourselves. I had no doubt that we would occasionally fail to live up to our own expectations.

SARAH REVERED SCHOOL SUPPLIES. A good pen, the right eraser, a stack of cunning Post-its in sherbet hues — these were the things worth having, the possessions that gave a girl a leg up on academics. We had gone to Staples every August since she was too small to need anything but a lunch bag and enthusiasm.

A week before the beginning of seventh grade, we made our annual pilgrimage. For the first time, it did not go well. We headed down the notebook aisle — we walked every aisle, even the ones with stuff she'd never need — and she stopped in front of the binder display. In years past she had bought one big binder and that was it, but she had heard rumors that the teachers at her new school wanted a binder for each subject.

"They should have given us more information about exactly what they want us to have," she said.

We settled for the things we were sure about — pens and pencils, but not the binders. As we headed out to the parking lot with not enough shopping bags, Sarah said, "This is usually a lot of fun, but not this time."

I called Lori, whose older daughter had already been through this, and she told me not to buy a thing. The anticipatory shopping ritual was as obsolete as ankle socks with ruffles. Teachers handed out supply lists on the first day of school; in middle school, supplies were task specific.

This information should have comforted us, but in fact it made matters worse. How vastly different would middle school be, if even the basic supply rules had changed? We were used to the rhythm of back-to-school, and all of a sudden what used to be helpful wasn't. We didn't quite know what to do, and the unknown made us apprehensive. Even Larry was a bit unsettled. When Sarah thought of a couple of items she had to have — a girl surely needed highlighters, even in this brave new world — he made a late-night run to Staples, and I imagine that it was to catch his breath as much as anything else.

A NEW SCHOOL held such promise. It was a fresh start — new friendships to strike, new teachers to impress, new teams to try out for, new food in the cafeteria, new school clothes, and oh, the sawdust aroma of freshly sharpened pencils. Since time and number two yellows began, the first day of school has been a big deal — and to top it off, Sarah was going to a girls' school, which meant that every single member of the incoming seventh grade was a potential pal. For an only child, it was heady stuff. She came downstairs on that first morning wearing an offhand air, but for once I knew what was up. Sarah had to pretend that she didn't care, or she'd fall down with desire.

She was ready to go ten minutes early, after what was undoubtedly the most nutritious breakfast she would have all year, and because this was such a big deal, Larry and I drove her to school together. We both wanted to see the look on her face when she got out of the car.

It fell somewhere between Cinderella at the ball and Bambi watching her beloved forest go up in flames.

TWO DAYS LATER the seventh graders had a half day of school, followed by a party at somebody's house who had a pool. The night before, I realized that Sarah didn't know I would be there.

"Listen," I said, "I just wanted you to know that I signed up to be a chaperone at the pool party. But I'll stay out of your way."

"Good," she replied.

"Which?" I asked.

"Both."

WOMEN WHO LIVE OR WORK TOGETHER eventually form a kind of tribe, based on the alpha gal and her menstrual cycle. The other women in the group realign their cycles until everyone is assured of not only empathy but a ready supply of Midol. They move through the universe as one.

They have nothing on the seventh graders, who came back from yet another of those wilderness bonding trips as though they had been living together since birth. They walked with the same nonchalant slouch, meant to cover the awful insecurity of being the youngest girls at school. They affected a heavy-lidded, appraising gaze when they stopped to talk, since they were terrified that everyone else was giving them the once-over. Even their voices changed. People made a big deal about boys' voices cracking and changing, but anyone with half an ear could hear it in girls, too. Their voices filled out and lost their warble. If a girl managed to avoid the cadence of "like, y'know, I go," she could fool a blindfolded listener into thinking she was an adult.

When I dropped Sarah off at school in the morning, I might as well have worn a sign that said OTHER on it. Most surprising of all, I would not have minded. Five hundred yammering girls was enough to rattle anyone. I felt like Tippi Hedren in the phone booth in *The Birds,* assaulted on all sides by shrieking seagulls. This was not conversation, at least not to me. This was hormones run amok, teenage girls temporarily freed from the authoritarian pressures of home and classroom. I was not eager to hang around, because I was so completely out of place.

Sarah loved her school. Every one of her teachers was possibly the most wonderful person on the planet, and the names of the new girls flew by so fast that I could not hope to keep track. Christinakimberlypaige was one terrific kid.

As for me, I was merely familiar. In the face of so much change, I retreated into the particulars of daily life, where I felt safe. I thought too much about exactly when the alarm clock ought to go off to get us out the door on time. I interrogated Sarah on whether she liked the lunch combinations that I had been packing for her for several years, and after she assured me that she did, I played Sally Field as grand inquisitor: Did she really, *really* love that pasta? I took refuge in stereotype. I micromanaged until I became the world's most boring mother. If God was truly in the details, then I was the pope.

"Mom," said Sarah, with a note of fear in her voice, "you have to stop."

She was absolutely right, which did not mean that it would be easy. In sixth grade I had nagged a little bit and told myself that we were addressing time management issues. This year I saw it for what it really was. Unwrap a nag, and there was a mother who hadn't yet made sense of the young woman who was her daughter — a mother who couldn't figure out who to be beyond useful. Nagging was not nagging. It was unresolved yearning, it was parenting in shards.

LARRY PICKED UP THE PHONE as Sarah and I rushed for the front door.

"Nancy wants to know if Sarah's going to school," he said. "Something about a plane crash in New York."

"Of course she's going," I said. "What does that have to do with us?"

We turned on the car radio, and by the time we got to the freeway, we had learned that people were capable of flying airplanes into large buildings full of other people. I turned at the entrance ramp, regardless. I drove to school because that was what I did at seven o'clock on a weekday morning. Under the circumstances, it struck me that I ought to do exactly what I always did.

The head of the upper school stood in the driveway to talk to parents as we dropped off our girls. He was a history teacher, which gave me odd comfort, since I figured that his point of view on the World Trade Center had more credibility than if he had taught algebra or coached the swim team. I wanted the voice of authority to tell me what to do.

"We're going to stay open," he said. "We feel that the girls will be well off together. The teachers are going to talk to them, and we're going to have an assembly to discuss what's happened." He held open the car door for Sarah. There were cars waiting behind me, so I did the numb, obedient thing — I told her I loved her and I let her go. Two blocks away, my heart tightened in a corkscrew and I started to cry. I looked at the faces in the cars coming toward me, and I could tell who had the radio on and who had a few moments of ignorant bliss remaining. There were far fewer of us applying mascara in the rearview mirror that morning. There were a lot of blank stares.

When I got home, Larry was standing in front of the television set.

I asked him, "Do you think she's safe there?"

He did. "They're not going to blow up her school or our house."

"Right. But what if they blow up a freeway between here and there? How are we going to get to her?"

What I really meant was, What if we cannot save her? It is every parent's subterranean lament, but it is supposed to surface on a predictable timetable: the first time a child stays away from home overnight, the first stint at sleep-away camp, the first plane flight alone, and then, fortissimo, the big split when they go off to college. From there, we fear with dwindling severity, as they marry, endure childbirth, and eat their meals without us around to fret about sufficient calcium intake. Eventually we trade places, and they fear for our safety. Our impotence is fairly easy to anticipate; the emotional trains usually run on time. Not today.

I grabbed my day's work and announced that I was going to drive back to the little business district near school, to wait until Sarah got out at 2:45. She was not getting on the school bus, not today. I had to be within sprinting distance, I had to be the one behind the wheel, as though proximity were any protection at all.

For the second time that day, I was at the door when the phone rang. It was the mother who sat one branch above me on the emergency phone tree, asking that I call the parents on my list to tell them that school was, in fact, closing for the day. I thought about letting Larry make the calls so that I could see Sarah sooner, but he drives much faster than I do — and after twenty years of fighting the freeways, he knows all the dodge routes on the surface streets. He would bring her home.

The first mom was already on the way to school when I reached her, and the second mom thanked me over and over again, as though the world was safer for my call. The third mom on my list sounded quite put out. She was the stepmother, as it turned out, and this week was the ex-wife's week to look after the girl in question, not hers. She already had a full day planned. I really ought to call the girl's mom, whose responsibility this was in the first place.

I got the mom's voice mail, and when I called the stepmom back I got her voice mail, too.

I left a message saying that I had not been able to reach the student's mother. Then I hung up and yelled, "So stop being such a spoiled brat, and go pick up your goddamn stepdaughter," at no one at all. I reported my failure to my phone-tree superior, who said she would make sure that someone at school kept calling. I tried not to think about the last girl left on a day like this, sitting by the driveway, waiting for someone who loved her to arrive.

When Sarah got home, she changed into her pajamas and requested special permission to watch a movie on a weekday. She picked *Tootsie,* where nobody died and true love triumphed in the end. Good people chased happiness and got it, in *Tootsie,* and the bad guy lost the girl. I ended up watching it with her, before I went back to watching the news.

FIVE NIGHTS LATER, which would have been my father's eightieth birthday, I dreamed that I would be dead by January. For some reason, I went to Sarah's orthodontist, who said that there was nothing he could do — either there wasn't enough medicine to go around or I was somehow expendable. He explained that many cases of tuberculosis were drug resistant.

"TB?" I said, in my dream. "I thought I had cancer."

"But the cancer's gotten smaller," said the orthodontist. "That's no problem. It's the TB."

At that I started to cry. "All I want is to see my daughter get older," I sobbed. "That's all. Just to know what Sarah's like when she's an adult." In my dream it had come to this: I was prepared to pack up every other wish I had ever had, if it meant I got to watch Sarah grow up.

The orthodontist became genuinely concerned, as though he had forgotten I had a child, and that made all the difference. "Don't worry, don't worry," he said, bustling around his office. "We'll take care of you. You're going to be fine."

Just like that, I was. I got the right medicine and I was cured, pulled back from the brink simply because I loved my daughter — unlike all the people who had been in the wrong place at the wrong time, days earlier. Love hadn't saved any of them, whether they loved their children, their parents, or anybody at all, and I woke up exhausted, not as pleased as I should have been by the way my dream had worked out. How was it possible to be happy? A dead man's wife had given birth to their child two days after the World Trade Center went down, and across the world, children danced in celebration in the street. Within ten miles of my house, there was a woman, whose name I forced myself to forget, who could not be bothered to pick up her husband's child. It was hard to feel anything but grim relief.

I had heard the notion that God could not be held responsible for our mortal, and moral, shortcomings. I had heard the notion that man could not grasp God's larger plan. No wonder I cast the orthodontist as God in my dream. The orthodontist made teeth line up to do the job they were designed to do. With a benign and compassionate air, with a firm and decisive hand, he ruled a finite universe made up of millimeters and brackets. There were no big surprises in the kingdom of orthodonture.

In the waking world, everything was up for grabs. Had it not been for the suicide flights, we might have rolled up to the central lesson of adolescence at a more manageable speed, but collision begets collision, and we had to face it before we were ready: There was no protecting Sarah, or anybody else, for that matter.

Even the most devoted parent is helpless, finally, and that is the pain that informs the small, stupid arguments we have with our children. We think we argue about grades, or wasted time, or a messy room, but that is all beside the point. Everything we ask of them boils down to one futile entreaty: Take care.

SARAH HAD A DREAM, TOO. Larry and I were bustling about, getting ready for a trip, but we did not plan to take her along. When she asked us where we were going, we said that we had to go put gasoline in the car before we left for Italy.

She got terribly upset, since we had never left her by herself in the house for an evening, let alone while we somehow managed to drive a car across the Atlantic Ocean. But no matter how hard she cried, we busied ourselves with our preparations — and when we were ready, Larry grabbed the car keys and we left her behind. She was completely on her own, and she did not want to be.

A MONTH LATER the girls were supposed to take a field trip to historic locales in downtown Los Angeles. Phyllis called me to discuss the relative importance of seeing a funicular railroad, when it required spending a day even farther away than school was, in one of Los Angeles's two prominent vertical neighborhoods. Without much conviction, I told her that Lori had said the girls ought to go, and we reminded each other that paralysis was no way to live.

But I had forgotten about tribal chat, and it turned out that the girls had been talking.

On the way to school on the day of the trip, Sarah asked, "What's anthrax, exactly?"

I heard the voice of her elementary school curriculum director, the one who was so adept at transgenerational chat: *Only answer the question they ask you. Don't give them more information than they can handle.* She was talking about sex, but I imagined that the same advice held for biological warfare.

"A bacteria."

"What does it do?"

"Makes you sick."

"How?"

"Well, you get it on your skin or breathe it, and it makes you sick."

"Really sick?"

"Really sick."

"Can you die?"

What a sad education.

"Yes."

"How does it start?"

"Like the flu."

I still listened for airplanes at night, but the younger crowd had moved on to worry about this generation's dangerous white powder. I tried to sound parental. "That's the good thing, see," I said. "Now people know that it starts like the flu, so if anybody feels like they have the flu, they can go to the doctor and get medicine."

"So there's something you can take."

"Yes, but nobody cares about sending anthrax to people like us, and . . ."

She cut me off. "You don't have to tell me that, Mom. It's okay."

We pulled up in front of school, where her classmates milled around, waiting to line up for the buses that would take them downtown. We were in plain sight, and I did not care.

"I'm going to embarrass you in front of your friends," I said.

She was amused. "Yeah? How?"

"I am going to kiss you good-bye before I let you out of the car."

She leaned her face toward me. I held that face in my hands, and then I gave her a kiss and let her go. Letting go was my new discipline. My instinct, everyone's instinct, was to hang on just a bit tighter, these days, to keep our children closer than we otherwise might. I was going to try not to give in to it.

On the Sidelines

THERE MUST BE A BETTER WAY TO SOCIALIZE GIRLS AND boys than to throw hundreds of them into a darkened, deafening gym, but the first middle school dance was a rite of passage. Sarah and Julia decided that the predance preparations would be much more fun if they did them together, so they spent the afternoon at our house and then headed up to Julia's to change into their party clothes. The combination of a new school and too much television news had sent both of them scurrying for the familiar, so they were pals again, the way they had been a couple of years before. But Julia already knew who she wanted to dance with that night, and Sarah's big concern seemed to be whether the refreshments would be any good. I wondered how long the alliance would hold.

I waited for a disagreement that never came, and by the time they were ready to go over to Julia's house, I had come to a realization that pleased me. Perhaps their friendship would survive in spite of their differences, and even flourish because of them. That was how lasting friendships were made, after all — not by being identical but by being together. They sought each other out every time there was a transition to be made, and they had a lot of history in common. They had seen each other at their worst and best and still made a date to get ready for the dance. That had to count for something in the long run.

I walked to the door with them, ready to watch while they headed up to Julia's house. We had, in our neighborhood, the occasional prostitute who wanted customers to have a quiet place to pull over instead of fighting for curb space on the nearby commercial street; we had a young guy who galvanized our dormant Neighborhood Watch group by screaming threats at women who walked by; we had a hardened wanderer or two who might give a couple of kids a hard time, so when the girls were little, we had gotten into the habit of escorting them to each other's houses. Then we settled for watching them, one parent at each end. Most recently, we had started calling as the girls left one house for the other.

"Want me to watch you walk up?" I offered.

"No, Mom." Sarah glanced at Julia and smiled. "We're big girls."

"Yeah, right," said Julia.

Sarah stuck her thumb in her mouth, which she had never done as a child. "See?"

They dissolved into a fit of giggles and ran up the block.

An hour before the dance, we headed over to Phyllis and Raphe's, along with another couple from the neighborhood whose daughter was joining our girls for the dance. With the rabid enthusiasm of paparazzi stalking a celebrity wedding, we pulled out our cameras and took pictures of the three girls together, testament to the wild range of adolescence: The outfits ranged from jeans and a

T-shirt to a glistening slip dress with heels, and Sarah was the only one wearing no makeup at all. The last time these three had looked so different from one another, they were dressed as Lucy, Desi, and Ethel Mertz for Halloween.

Before they left, I took Sarah aside for a moment.

"Look, I have to say something to you, and I feel like an idiot for saying it, but if I don't and something happens I'll feel like a worse idiot, so there you are," I said.

She tried very hard not to laugh. "Mom, whatever it is you're going to say, you don't have to worry."

I wasn't worried about her. I was worried about kids I'd never met.

"There are going to be lots of kids you don't know at the dance," I said. "You do not take an open drink from anyone, even from someone you know. Soda in a can. That's it. "

"Okay," she said. She actually seemed pleased that I'd thought to mention it.

She came home as fed up as she had been excited only hours before. It was way too hot, way too loud, there were way too many people and way more girls than boys. Even if it had been cool and quiet and a smaller crowd, there would have been little chance of dancing with anyone — not that she wanted to, anyhow. Two girls she knew got into a spat over the last dance with a particular boy who had either preferred or been monopolized by one of them, depending on which girl was telling the story. So much for the joys of young romance. Sarah reported that she did not intend to attend the second school dance, in the spring.

I said silent thanks for my Philadelphia friend, who came out to California every summer with her son, who was almost three years older than Sarah. They always had a free weekend before he started basketball camp, and we always drove up the coast to see them. No peers, no need to be cool, so the kids dove for quarters in the pool and ate guacamole and chips. It struck me as a much easier way to get acclimated to the opposite sex.

NOT EVERY CHILD is so reluctant. Like any mother who is conscious and has two working ears, I have heard stories about oral sex on the preteen party circuit. The best urban legend (and let us pray that is what it is) involves parents who choose short tablecloths instead of the traditional floor-length ones for their child's bat mitzvah, so that nobody can hide underneath the table. There have been rumors of oral sex on the chartered bus between the temple and the party that followed the service — anyplace, in fact, where a boy and a girl had five unsupervised minutes together. President Clinton succeeded in redefining sex not just for himself but for the next generation of voters: Oral sex has replaced untucking a girl's blouse as the cool thing that boys insist there is no reason not to do.

It would be comforting to dismiss all of this as the hysterical imaginings of overbearing parents, but adults who had the nerve to broach the subject found otherwise: One psychologist told the *New York Times* about the sixth, seventh, and eighth graders who said that they were virgins and then confessed that they had had oral sex fifty or sixty times. Another psychologist called it "body-part sex," performed with a "casual, brazen attitude." A federally financed study estimated that half of all teenage boys had had oral sex — which meant either that a small group of girls had been extremely busy or that oral sex was, in fact, endemic among youngsters whose judgment was considered suspect by every major bureaucracy from the Department of Motor Vehicles to the banks that handed out retail credit cards.

Parents are supposed to be comforted by the fact that teenage intercourse is on the decline, and I am, even though that is kind of like being happy that your kid sticks to beer instead of tequila shots. We are supposed to ignore the fact that the age at first intercourse continues to get younger with every decade because at least the statistical pool is shrinking. If the pregnancy rate is down, though, it is not because girls have found hobbies. They simply have better access to birth control — or their boyfriends have encouraged them to find new ways to express their affection.

And so, back to oral sex, which for the current generation essentially means the gratification of young men by young women. It used to be something that required an existing level of intimacy; now it is the equivalent of a calling card in an Edith Wharton novel. It is considered "safe and fun and a prelude to intercourse, where it used to be the other way around," a specialist in adolescent medicine told the *Times*. We have successfully terrorized our children with stories of unwanted pregnancies and sexually transmitted diseases, but there seems to be no stopping them. They have simply taken their collective libido on an unexpected detour. It seems to me the sexual equivalent of having dessert before the meal. How can a parent who sees the sexual universe one way hope to advise a daughter who sees it the other way around?

My friend Lori liked abstinence. It was as straightforward as a superhighway. Once a girl embraced virginity, she could — she should — breeze right past moral cloverleafs like oral sex. Hummie, whose Sarah was a year older than Lori's eldest, preferred a more pragmatic approach based on the statistical likelihood that none of our daughters would be virgins by the time they graduated from college. He told his daughter that he or Vicky would rather she carry condoms in her purse than be unprepared when passion struck — as they were sure, at some point, it would.

Lori rejected Hummie's position as a tacit endorsement of teen sex. Hummie figured that Lori's philosophy, however well-intentioned, left her daughters in the lurch. I yearned to embrace Lori's absolutist stance, but I could not, since we were talking about decisions that got made in the heat of the moment — and since I, for one, had not managed to get to twenty-one with my virginity intact. How could I expect more of my daughter than I did of myself?

Yes, I wanted Sarah to wait until she was old enough to be in love, and yes, I thought that ought to come after the car keys and with luck after she declared her college major, but that's what I wanted and what I thought. What she wanted and thought was out there on the horizon somewhere — and to be honest, I would be sad if Sarah thought of me and my advice just as the first love of her life wrapped his arms around her and turned out to be a great kisser. Forget sad. I would think she was nuts.

I did speak up once, as we drove past a billboard advertising a television program that promised a rather predatory and detached look at sex. "Now that's a shame," I said, keeping my eyes on the road.

But I was afraid to preach abstinence because that would make sex a handy tool for rebellion. I was afraid to preach abstinence because if Sarah disagreed, she would have a hard time coming to me to talk about it.

I had no such fear about preaching sexual politics. What drove me crazy about tween oral sex, aside from its rampancy, was the lack of reciprocity. Not that I wanted thirteen-year-old girls to be on the receiving end; no, I wanted everyone to take one giant step backward and invest any kind of sex with the intimacy it deserved. Since nobody wanted to hear that, I felt compelled to point out the inequity of the current arrangement to any parent who would listen. Decades after the sexual revolution and the birth control pill gave women a measure of bedroom equality, we were back to the double standard.

* * *

IT WAS FUN to conflate statistics, to fold them over each other like egg whites into a cake batter. While the girls were at the dance, I had time to think about some of the things I had learned:

Depending on which study I chose to believe, girls shopped at least once a week, and possibly an average of fifteen times each month.

By the time they were sixteen, girls complained that they had no spare time for physical activities like team sports.

Girls who participated in athletics were less likely to be sexually active.

Were they less sexually active because their bodies were otherwise engaged? Or were they less sexually active because they spent less time buying the sort of clothing that titillated even the wearer? Did shopping somehow lead to sex? In either case, a girl might just be looking for something or someone to make her feel special. It didn't matter: If we could get more girls out of the mall and onto the playing field, early sex might become as passé as last year's boy band.

A FEW DAYS LATER, I was standing in line at a coffee place behind a woman for whom nothing on the lengthy menu was exactly right. She was the reason that people outside Los Angeles make fun of us: She micromanaged her soy, half-caff, dry, extra-hot, double-cup latte until I wanted to hold her under the drip spigot and make her drink it plain. All this while she negotiated with the person at the other end of her cell phone to pick up Lisa at ballet class. She was toned; she had not only a yoga mat but also one of those cunning tubular bags to hold it. I sneered and judged her a selfish mom.

And what would she think when she turned and saw me, fresh from the horse, wearing filthy jeans, a stained T-shirt, and no makeup? I had grime under my fingernails. If we were going to trade surface assumptions, she had every right to dismiss me as one of those women who just didn't care anymore.

Racial profiling is enough to lose a public official his support, if not his job, but mom profiling has always been a sanctioned indoor sport. When our daughters are young, we get the benefit of the doubt — short of screaming at a girl for getting paint on her shirt or complaining publicly about her eating habits, the mother of a young girl is by definition a good mom, just as all pregnant women are radiant.

Once those girls hit adolescence, though, a mother's performance is anybody's business. For all I knew, the woman in front of me was a brain surgeon who yesterday had saved two lives. For all she knew, I cleaned up pretty good. Ah, but if we gave mothers a break, then stand-up comics and sitcom writers would go begging.

ROCKY HAD GONE LAME days before the first school-league horse show in the fall, but Sarah was determined to participate, so she spent an entire day waiting around for the chance to ride a borrowed horse in one of the four classes in her division — the flat class, which required only the walk, trot, and canter, no jumping. Rocky held his health for the second show, in December, but he failed to communicate in advance his dislike of the pink plastic flowers that were twined around one of the little jumps. He waited until he was right in front of that jump, in the warm-up round, and then he balked and tossed Sarah to the ground. To make matters worse, I ran right over to make sure that she was all right.

It was an incomprehensible humiliation, and it was all my fault. Meredith was not there, though Sarah would never have blamed her trainer. Meredith's young assistant was too much of a role model for Sarah to risk alienating her. Larry rarely got closer than a carrot's length to Rocky. I was the only logical target.

As soon as we got Rocky back into his stall, Sarah stormed away from me in a steamy cloud of tears, spewing complaints as she went. I should have put a more experienced rider on him for the warm-up round. I somehow should have made sure that there were no witnesses, even though there were hundreds of people milling around. Why weren't we already in the car, heading home? She was not getting back on that stupid horse, and why hadn't I gotten her out of there by now?

She hid out at the end of a bank of stalls and waited for me to make the world right. I dealt my mom cards one by one.

"Everybody falls off," I said, "but I guess that doesn't make it any easier when it happens to you."

She shot me a venomous look, so I tried for a more authoritative approach. Girls fell off in Meredith's lessons in the canyon and got back on, and Sarah still had four rounds of competition ahead of her. I knew, with a clarity that often eluded me in the real world, exactly what was supposed to happen next.

"Sarah, I know you're upset, but you have to get back on the horse. That's what Meredith would say if she were here."

More tears. How dare I try to channel Meredith, who would have spared Sarah this embarrassment in the first place, because she would have known just how frightening pink plastic flowers can be.

"I am not getting back on," she said, turning her back and heading for the parking lot. "I am not going to get back on. You don't understand at all."

There it was, the crux of adolescence, the almost religious faith in a parent's ability to get nothing right. From the way she said it, I knew there was no point in hauling out my own humiliation credentials; no need to mention the mistake in the first four bars of the Chopin piece that had required starting all over, in front of a row of Chicago all-school competition judges. No need to tell her about the moment when I and my beautiful prom dress turned to the right, and the strapless bra stayed put, which meant that half of the bra was now under my arm and half of me was no longer inside the bra. There was no way to convince her that I understood — not even if I had once fallen off an identical horse in front of an identical jump. At that moment, I had no credibility.

I also had no hot coffee, no crossword with a nice sharp pencil, no quiet Sunday at home with the newspaper. I had been up since 4:30 in the morning, one sweater shy of warm, dust between my teeth, all for the opportunity to be told that I was less helpful than a rock.

I could have answered in kind. I could have said, "Fine. If I don't understand, then you figure it out for yourself," and stomped off in a huff, but that would only have prolonged the agony. And she had to get back on the horse, or I'd have Meredith mad at me as well. It was my job to see that she did — even though I was fairly terrified that she would.

Let go, let go, let go.

"Sarah," I said, "nothing I have said is doing any good here, but I am trying to figure out what will. All I know is, you have to figure out some way to get back on that horse if you want to continue riding for the team. You cannot come to school shows if you do not get back on the horse."

"How can you say that?" she said. "Of course I'm going to ride for the team." She stormed off in yet another direction, and I hung back and waited.

After about ten minutes, she sidled quietly back into public view, in the sandy area between the rings. Then a wondrous thing happened. One by one, her teammates from school approached her, each one with a story that began, "Did I ever tell you about the time . . . ?" I stood to the side and listened as they described an array of embarrassments, from falling off to forgetting which jump was next. Girls who rode with Sarah in the canyon came over to her as well. Wherever the wretched adolescent girls we hear about were that day, they were not at the school-league horse show, where compassion ran high.

Sarah's mouth stopped quivering, and she tried on a very small smile. She came over and asked me to help with the hair net that each girl had to wear under her helmet. She got back on Rocky. Finally it was her turn to ride the first hunter course, which involved cantering around the ring and jumping a bunch of jumps, including the one with the pink flowers. It was her first jumping class ever. I turned my back to the ring and held on to Larry's arm.

"Just tell me if she gets around," I said.

She did; I peeked. She came out with glistening eyes and hugs and kisses for me, for Larry, for Rocky. It was dark out by the time they called her last class of the day, the flat class, and no one would have faulted her if she had skipped it and gone home early, as some of the girls did. Instead, she went around under the lights, smiling, victorious without a single ribbon. I was inordinately proud — and aware that the girls had said pretty much what I had said, except that Sarah was willing to listen to it from them.

It was not my job to make sure that Sarah got back on Rocky, I told myself. It was my job to hold steady, while she figured it out for herself.

We were entering the phase when a mother's opinion was suspect for the very reason that it used to be gospel — because she is a mother. Experts who disagree on everything else agree that it is inevitable — Judith Harris, who says that peers, not parents, define personality; Lyn Brown, who says that rejection is an essential part of separation; author Rosalind Wiseman, who spends her working life listening to teens.

I had to admit that it made perfect sense. If Sarah didn't respect what her friends said, that would mean that she didn't respect girls, which included herself, which would make me even less happy than being ignored.

I THOUGHT WE HAD WRAPPED a ribbon around the day, so I was not prepared for Meredith's response when I told her about the flowered-jump debacle.

"She needs a better horse," said Meredith.

21

Sea Changes

SOME OF THE SEVENTH-GRADE GIRLS CAME FROM SCHOOLS that stressed drill and performance, and they sailed into semester exams, at the end of January, like seasoned pros. Some of the girls, like Sarah, came from schools that preferred not to burden those birdlike shoulders with the pressure of grades and scores. Phyllis and I used to joke that all the girls got identical paragraphs of praise in their twice-yearly evaluations. Our elementary school was designed primarily to make the kids feel good about themselves.

The first ninety-minute Latin test of Sarah's short life accomplished exactly the opposite. The test went on forever, at least in Sarah's frame of reference, and it seemed to include only things that she had not studied, although she had studied everything. Thanks to the priceless self-esteem that had been so carefully nurtured for the first ten years of her life, she had never anticipated trouble; as such, she was demolished by her bad grade. She did great in class — so was she a champ, or was she a failure?

Larry and I were not used to grades either. I might have gotten mired in a pointless discussion of the relationship between grades and self-image had Larry not seen the easy solution.

"Flash cards," he said, the only one of us who had survived high school Latin. I thought to myself that this, not the mechanics of sperm and egg, was the reason to have a dad around. We give men grief for not being in touch with their feelings, but there are times when a nice, detached practicality is a big help. Introspection is a fine thing, but not after one Latin test. We embraced flash cards as a family philosophy and went back about our business.

WHEN TO SPEAK UP, and what to say, were clearly the big issues for us. I had kept quiet now for a semester and change, while Sarah hung out with a group of girls who treated her, eerily, the way the vinyl-purse group of girls had treated me when I was in the seventh and eighth grades. They admired her studious nature even as they loudly proclaimed their lack of interest in grades, and they kept her close because she was industrious, willing to go grab a soda, or to explain an algebra problem. I imagined that she liked them because they were easygoing, sociable girls. I knew how this would likely end, because I knew how it ended for me: I still remembered the Saturday afternoon when the lead girl, Babs, announced in front of everyone that they didn't want to hang around with me anymore. But I couldn't say that, not even if I was careful to explain that I was glad, in retrospect, to have been dumped. No one wanted to hear her mother predict rejection.

To my eye, Sarah's old friends were having an easier time of assimilation. Phyllis and Julia regularly argued about how much time

Julia spent on the phone. Aviva had jock buddies. Emily spent her time with incipient class officers and budding stars of the stage. The front-row moms were concerned: Lori wanted to know why Sarah hadn't found more appropriate friends, and Phyllis and Jo Ann asked, offhandedly but fairly often, if Sarah ever mentioned anyone new.

In the time-honored tradition of rulers whose power had begun to erode, they wanted me to take a stand. I could issue an edict: No more hanging around with those girls; find some friends your father and I like better. It sounded like my parents weighing in on a college boyfriend of mine, an impossibly handsome fellow who couldn't decide if his brains or his money bored him more. They let me know at every possible turn that he was not good enough for their daughter, and in response I stuck with him far longer than I might have if they'd kept their mouths shut.

I had resented their lack of faith in my judgment. Sarah might reasonably resent us, if we started hounding her. There was no danger here beyond the possibility that for a few weeks she would ingest more high-fructose corn syrup than we might like because of all those sodas. I had the luxury of time; I could afford not to meddle.

"I just have to be patient," I said to Lori. "She'll grow out of it."

"Do you think she'll grow out of it?" I asked Larry. He looked at me with a mix of bewilderment and fear. He had gone to all-boys schools until he went to college; I might as well consult a Sherpa guide about the nuances of adolescent female friendship. I retreated, and waited, and hoped that we were doing the right thing by doing nothing at all.

NEWS OF SARAH'S LIBERATION came thirdhand, from Aviva to Jo Ann to me. Aviva came home one day and reported to her mother that Sarah had done what Aviva considered to be "a very brave thing." Sarah had sat down at her regular seat at her regular table for lunch, and then something made her change her mind. She got up and moved to a different table, which in the world of adolescent girlhood was the equivalent of handing in your resignation and decamping to the competition.

There would be no going back, since the cachet of any one group depended on its refusal to take back members who had strayed. That was what Aviva admired — Sarah's willingness to give up her security blanket to sit with girls who seemed like a better match.

So I knew, because Jo Ann told me, but I didn't know, because Sarah hadn't mentioned it. I picked up Sarah at the bus stop after school and drove her over to ride Rocky. Halfway there, she still hadn't said anything.

"Aviva told her mom that you switched tables at lunch," I said, the epitome of offhandedness. "I think she was impressed."

"Yeah," she said, matching me cool for cool. "I decided I didn't want to sit there anymore."

"So who'd you sit with instead?"

"Some girls."

THE DECISION TO JETTISON her friends was not the only sea change of seventh grade. Homework took precedence over practicing the piano. Riding Rocky took precedence over practicing the piano. And finally, eating, sleeping, taking a shower, and hitting tennis balls for the dog to chase took precedence over practicing the piano.

Larry computed what else we might do with the money we spent renting the piano, but I refused to call the company to have it taken away. Everyone this side of a prodigy — including me — had at some point given up the piano, only to regret it years later. I pushed, and Sarah resisted, and then I offered her a stopgap compromise: She and I could share the weekly time slot, so she would only have to practice for two lessons a month instead of four. I would take piano lessons for the first time in almost forty years.

She was so relieved that she said yes. One night, after dinner, she went into the front bedroom that served simultaneously as her homework space, our guest room, and the equine equipment storage closet. As she settled in, she called out, "What are you doing, Mom?"

"Just finished the dishes. Maybe I'll take a look at the paper."

"You should practice the piano."

I practiced. Sarah's teacher was one of those saints who understood that people practiced more if they got to play pieces they liked, so she had found me a simplified version of a Scott Joplin rag, just the main theme, with everything stripped away but the melody line and a couple of two-note chords. When I could play that without stopping, I tackled the real arrangement, chunk by chunk, flats and sharps and naturals and some notes that I pretended weren't there.

We got into a routine: Most nights, Sarah started in on her homework and I played "Bethena's Waltz." Every other week, I was ready for my lesson and she was not. Finally we told the teacher that we would not be taking lessons anymore, but we kept the piano, and I played while she did her homework. Sometimes she came out of her room, stood behind me with her hands on my shoulders, and told me to use just a little more pedal.

CAROLYN BROUGHT A DATE to this year's seder. Poor guy. We were a tough crowd, protective, curious, and one by one we made our way over to check him out. Even my mother gave him the once-over, just as years ago my sister and I had evaluated Allen, then known as "that guy Al," the man who wanted to marry my mom. I caught Sarah looking at Carolyn's date from the kids' table. Not that it was any of our business — but he was a new idea, and we wanted to figure out what he meant.

As though we could. Traditional narrative built reassuringly to a climax and a resolution, as anyone who had sat through high school English lit could tell you. The most profitable subcategory was the Hollywood action movie, where Matt Damon or Harrison Ford would almost certainly not die; we got the thrill of life without any of the usual anxiety about its outcome. Extraneous events — the stuff that filled offscreen lives — ended up on the cutting-room floor. Traditional narrative was efficient.

Real life didn't happen in three acts. President Clinton's story was about the boy who pulled himself up by his dusty bootstraps to become a beloved president — until he had a midlife crisis and the story galloped off in a whole new direction. Was the presidency the second act? Was Monica the stunning denouement? It was too soon to tell. Life folded back on itself like an origami bird. The small, insignificant moment could turn out to be a watershed, but we would not know for years to come.

Structured stories held us close and pointed to the big moments. Life, in comparison, was pretty elusive. There was no violin section to let us know that this was an important scene — and in truth, most of us never encountered an apocalypse. We got lots of little moments, regular moments, in which a new guy came to dinner or a daughter told her mom to practice the piano, and it was up to us to see that they mattered.

Carolyn said that traditional narrative was a male invention, but I don't think she said it to bash men who wrote. I think she said it to suggest that there were other stories worth telling, stories whose spine did not extend in a predictable direction. This would be the first and last time that guy came to a seder, but we were not supposed to know, not yet. Sarah would turn out to be whoever she turned out to be, but we were not supposed to know that either.

AN OBJECTIVE OBSERVER would conclude that Sarah was the most improved rider on the school equestrian team, because she began the season by falling off her horse and ended it with ribbons in two classes. In the weeks before the spring sports banquet, she broached the subject frequently, and I listened as she analyzed who among the other riders might qualify for the year-end honors. She had hunches about the other categories — most dedicated rider, most valuable rider — but every time she thought about most improved, she came to the startling conclusion that she might well be it.

The honor came with a plaque. On the day the team members voted, Sarah voted for someone else.

"Honey, why did you do that?"

"I don't know. It felt funny to vote for myself."

"First rule of elections," I said. "If you don't think you're worth voting for, why should anybody else?"

She hadn't thought of that.

"It's okay," she said, in a bad impersonation of someone who didn't care. "I'm not going to not win by one vote."

The night of the banquet, she was adamantly cool, chatting with a teammate while the parents complimented each other on how nice we looked in civilian clothes. She was fine, in fact, until the teams split up for their individual meetings and she found herself sitting with her teammates at a conference table in one of the school offices, surrounded by parents, staring at a pile of gift-wrapped awards.

One of the team sponsors consulted a printout of the year's statistics.

"Our most improved rider started out the season by falling off her horse," she said, and Sarah fairly vibrated with hope. She wasn't sure yet; someone else might have fallen off. When the woman said, "but she ended up at the last show with a fifth place and an eighth place," Sarah knew that the team had voted the award to her. She reached for the little plaque with trembling fingers and a speechless smile, and we all applauded.

Suddenly she was on her feet to help hand out the rest of the prizes, animated, cracking wise. I was amazed at the change in her. Researchers would say she was happy because she was involved in athletics, but that wasn't all of it. She had become a member in good standing of the equestrian team; she had made what the other girls considered to be a valuable contribution, and she had the plaque to prove it. An only child with precious few relatives had found a big group she wanted to belong to, and she had worked hard and had been made to feel welcome. It was a moment of no significance outside that room, and I doubted I had ever seen her happier.

A Stall of One's Own

WE HAD TO BUY A HORSE.

This was dangerous terrain. I did not utter those words aloud at first, because I knew that the only safe fantasy was a private one. You don't tell someone you love them unless you're prepared to deal with the consequences; I couldn't tell an obsessed twelve-year-old and an amenable dad that we needed a horse unless I was prepared to have them say okay. Parents divide up the various provinces of daily life, based on their expertise. Larry was in charge of making sure we were optimistic and drove the appropriate cars. I oversaw dark leafy greens and not letting the horse thing get too crazy.

So I kept the notion of buying a horse to myself, until Rocky's owners informed me that they intended to double the price of his lease for the coveted summer months. In six weeks, an overweight, marginally sound horse would cost almost as much as our monthly mortgage payment, and he would require more upkeep than the house that mortgage paid for. Once the price went up, it would probably not come down.

I felt like a chump. Kibitzers in the canyon confirmed my own harsh appraisal of the situation, which was that it was crazy. More than one of them told me that we could own a horse for less.

Once they said it, I could not help but think the proposition through. That was the problem: I figured out a way to rationalize insanity. If we found a cheap horse and amortized the purchase price over our life with the horse — which would end the day Sarah left for college — then owning a horse would be cheaper than leasing one. I did not address the question of how to find a cheap horse that was in any better shape than Rocky was. I left that to magic.

Gingerly, I informed Larry of my opinion. He recoiled. I reassured him that this was not half as crazy as it sounded, because we would actually be saving money in the long run. Besides, I was willing to set a price ceiling that would guarantee us a spavined wreck — in which case we could say we'd looked and retire the whole idea. In the meantime — magic again — a cheaper lease horse surely would appear on the scene.

BABY BOOMERS STAND at a very crowded crossroads: Our carpe diem approach to life has gotten us into fun stuff like the sexual revolution and California what's-fresh-this-minute cuisine, but it has also gotten us into a particular kind of trouble. We are about to pay quite literally for our good times. The government estimates that half of us will fail to save enough to retire at sixty-five, by a long shot — instead, we will run out of money an average of nineteen years too soon. Most baby boomers will never be able to retire unless we get a job running a movie studio tomorrow, no later, with a huge golden parachute payment if we have to bail.

The math is sadly easy: Expected income times remaining work years does not yield a sufficiently large nest egg. There is no carrot dangling at the end of the stick, no matter how hard we try. Under the circumstances, maybe the only thing left is an existential shrug.

Larry and I had sought out an investment counselor long before horses became an issue to see if we would ever have enough savings to do whatever it is that people with enough savings do. The first candidate was blunt: The only way to reach our financial goals was to do without. His list of expendables included virtually everything we had worked so hard to be able to afford, including family vacations anywhere that required an overnight stay, and a car new enough to have front air bags, if not side. The second candidate said that the unhappiest client he ever had drove an ancient car, lived in a studio apartment, had a huge retirement account, and dropped dead unexpectedly before he could spend a penny of it. We went back to doing the best we could.

We both worried about the finances of horse ownership, but Larry worried even more about the long-term consequences. The canyon didn't have a fancy barn with a support staff, which meant that we would be responsible for the horse seven days a week, rain or shine. We were stretched pretty thin already, and we had Rocky only three days a week. Larry couldn't help but wish that we'd gotten Sarah interested in something where she could more easily be self-sufficient.

"Remind me again," he said, "why we didn't buy her a chess set."

This would be easier, I said, if we thought of the horse as a twelve-hundred-pound metaphor with hooves. He was whatever parents did that they had never intended to do, because it mattered more to their child than anything. He was that unexpected stretch in an unlikely direction, because it was where a kid wanted to go. In someone else's family, the horse might in fact be a chess set, or a baseball mitt, or a sewing machine. In someone else's family, no longer in ours, he might be a piano.

He was the place we would not be if Sarah hadn't wanted so badly to be there. The time to say no was years past, back before we ever put her on a pony in the first place. We could have picked something else to do — but once we let her ride, it seemed to me that we had a responsibility to keep her riding as long as she wanted to, as long as we could. We had to make every effort. Our choice was either to grouse about it or to embrace it and see where we ended up.

We would have to give up any thought of home improvement, of impulse purchases, of fancier cookware or an automatic sprinkler system. As much as I wanted all of those things, I was prepared to defer them. After Sarah's next lesson, I moseyed over to Meredith.

"Larry and I were thinking," I said, "that at some point in the future we might want to consider whether to look for a horse for Sarah."

She smiled. She saw right through "some point," and "might" and "whether." Although I was scared, I smiled back. I had no idea what we were getting into, and I did not much care. Having led a premeditated life until that exact moment in time, I slid over into the passenger seat and let Fate take the wheel.

MEREDITH SAID, "The first rule of buying a horse is: Never, ever buy the first horse you see. You'll fall in love with the first horse you see, but it's not necessarily the horse. You're in love with the idea of owning a horse. If you keep that in mind, we can start to look."

We told Sarah that we were curious to see what was out there and that we had no expectation of finding anything in our price range. If nothing else, we would come away at peace with Rocky's inflated price tag. We said it could take a year, if we found anything at all, but we were happy to look at the various Web sites that offered horses for sale. For her part, she seemed quite thrilled just to look.

Meredith surfed the Web and called around, and a couple of weeks later Sarah and I set off very early in the morning to visit a sale barn with Meredith and another girl and her mom. A sale barn was exactly that, a place where people sent their horses to be sold, and amazingly, they had a horse in our price range that was still breathing.

Sarah and the other girl walked to the stalls with the owner, and when they returned I had to stifle a laugh. Sarah, the far smaller of the two girls, was walking the far larger of the two horses, a big, dark brown horse with none of the cunning white markings that undoubtedly cost extra. He was just a big, dark brown horse, and I was frankly underwhelmed. Meredith gave him the once-over and whispered to me, "He's gorgeous."

A chill ran down my spine as I realized the vastness of my ignorance.

"He hasn't done anything yet," I said.

"If he's as good moving as he is standing still, you're in trouble," she said.

He was. After a half hour of watching Sarah ride, I began to think that we had stumbled upon a bargain. I said something effusive about Lucky Penny, or whatever his name was, to the barn owner, who shot me a pitying smile. That horse, the one we had come to see, had been sold two days ago. This horse was named Reno, and he was a tad pricier. Much nicer, of course, but pricier.

By the end of the morning, Meredith was in love with him, Sarah was in love with him, and I had become the villain of the piece. "He's too expensive for us," I said. The barn owner immediately discounted him 15 percent.

"He's too expensive for us," I repeated, and we piled into the car. The other girl, who had more money to spend, felt sorry for Sarah, which only made things worse.

Since Meredith was in love with the horse, she chose not to take me seriously. For a week the irresistible force bumped against the immovable object: She said he was perfect, and I complained about his age, his size, and the price. When all else failed, I threw her own edict back at her: Never, ever buy the first and only horse you see.

We went back with Larry to see him a second time, which only convinced Meredith that someone with more sense than Sarah's parents was going to grab him any second. Finally she snapped at me, "Just pretend he's the ninth or tenth horse you saw and write the check. Think of all the money you'll save not looking anymore."

She was too crafty for me. If we could get the owners to come down in price, we would not have to spend money looking at nine or ten other horses — not a penny on doctor visits to ensure that a horse was healthy, not a nickel on gasoline, nothing. We would not have to take Rocky's summer lease, which was a three-month, all-or-nothing deal. If we could spend a bit more than we had originally intended, we would save a great deal.

We brought Reno up to the canyon over the Memorial Day weekend, to see how he behaved in a new setting. Like a prince. We trailered him to an equine medical center to see if he had a deal-breaking ailment or injury. He did not. I had hoped for divine intervention, some unexpected glitch that would end our dream of horse ownership, but the only remaining issue was the gap between what we wanted to spend and what the owners wanted to get.

I called the woman who owned the sale barn and asked how low an offer I could make and get a bargaining response instead of a flat-out no. The figure she quoted was more than our budget but not that much more, so I made the offer. The owners came down in price, in response, but not as much as I had come up. There was still a sizable gap. I could not in good conscience say yes.

"I'll have to talk to Larry," I said. "I don't think we can do it." I didn't have to talk to Larry. I knew absolutely that we couldn't do it, but I wasn't prepared to admit it quite yet. I convinced myself that we could float Rocky for a couple of months while we figured out what to do. I congratulated myself on not caving in to desire.

Ten minutes later the phone rang. The woman from the sale barn had called Reno's owner and told her she was crazy not to sell us the horse, that he and Sarah were a great pair, that in three days the owner would owe the sale barn another month's fees, and if she subtracted that amount from her price, plus a little bit more, this would all be over. At our price.

The woman from the sale barn wanted to know: Would I rather send a check, or simply wire the money directly into her account?

LARRY'S OFFICE IS IN THE BASEMENT and mine is right above it, at the back of the house. I went downstairs to tell him that we owned a horse, and then he followed me up to the little hallway at the head of the basement stairs. I stepped over to make room for him next to me, but he chose instead to stand right behind me on the top step. Clinging to the stair railing seemed to help his financial vertigo. I called to Sarah, who was doing her homework in the front room, and asked her to join us.

"Sarah, stand right there," I said, "so we can both see your face."

"What is it?" she said, a bit irked at being taken away from her homework.

"He's yours," I replied.

She was shaking when she hugged me, and then she had to jump up and down, and hug Larry, and hug me again, and run around thc house. We drove over to the stalls just long enough for her to hug Reno, too, and then we drove back home.

REACTIONS TO THE NEWS varied along gender lines.

"That's nuts," said a man who could afford to own a horse and retire, simultaneously. Horses depreciated, and there was upkeep along the way. He did not understand why anyone would make an investment that was guaranteed to lose money.

"It's not an investment," I said. "It's a horse."

"Crazy," said another guy, who had a built-in wine cellar in his house.

"Yep," I said.

Carolyn was not a spendthrift by any means, but she did not regard life as a series of investments either.

"Valiant," she said.

Aviva, whose weekends were crammed full of art lessons and tennis practice, managed to find an afternoon to meet Reno and watch Sarah take a lesson. Emily, who had no interest in horses, came out to meet him anyway. Julia's younger sister, who liked horses, was so overwhelmed to meet Reno that she drew a picture of him for Sarah, to commemorate the event. The girls on the equestrian team congratulated her and asked to see a photograph.

And those were people who already knew us. Virtual strangers in the canyon lent us bridles and offered advice, and the girls in

Meredith's lesson treated Sarah as though she were the luckiest girl on earth. At that moment in time, she was. We ordered a nameplate for the stall:

RENO
Owner: Sarah Dietz

There was some initial confusion when I called to place the order, because my credit card was under my last name, but I wanted Sarah's last name, which was Larry's, on the stall plate. The young woman who took the order wanted to know how they ought to file the invoice — under *S* or under *D?*

"*S,*" I said warily. Last year I had been unable to locate Sarah's social security number because I'd filed it with Larry's number, under *L.*

When I repeated the conversation to one of the other canyon moms, she gave me a piece of advice.

"You'd be better off being Mrs. Dietz, just in the canyon," she said. "It would make things easier. Isn't that what the girls call you?"

In fact they did, no matter how often I told them to call me Karen or explained that I used my last name, not Larry's. So I became Mrs. Dietz in the canyon, having not been Mrs. Dietz, anywhere, for the first seventeen years of our marriage. The canyon was Sarah's world; she was at the center of it, not us, and I was significant only in reference to her. Every time I turned left off Sunset Boulevard, toward the stalls and the riding rings, I left my usual self behind, and I became a horseback mom. Karen Dietz. Mrs. Dietz. One-third of "the Dietzes."

That was a change worth noting. Sarah had been our daughter for years — through all of those meals with too many adults, through endless introductions to people we knew from work, on trips that Larry and I planned because a six-, or eight-, or even ten-year-old was not yet a fully vested member of the family. She had voting rights, but we had veto power. In the canyon the momentum had shifted. This was Sarah's part of the story. We existed in relation to her, as she used to in relation to us.

The markers by which most people knew me meant nothing there. Thanks to Sarah, I had a dual identity. I had the odd opportunity that so many midlifers wished for, the chance to re-create myself, or at least half of myself.

IN THE DAYS THAT FOLLOWED Reno's arrival, mothers of older girls approached me to welcome the newest member of their sorority. They told me I would never have a free moment again, as though I had had lots of them before now. They told me to get heavy boots in case Reno stepped on my toe. They said that Sarah would be filthier than I could possibly imagine. They agreed that this was the best bad decision any of them had ever made.

"Better here," one of them said, "than at the mall."

There was no way to know, back then, but Reno was going to leave my genteel dream of horseback riding in the dust. He would carry Sarah into a far more complicated world, where people knew the difference between a simple lead change and a flying change and expected her to do the one she'd been asked to do, a place where people memorized slogans like "Rise and fall with the leg on the wall" because it turned out there was a wrong time to have one's seat out of the saddle at the posting trot. There were patterns to learn and a proper length of rein, gaits and extended gaits, and ten times more. There was a correct number of strides between one jump and the next.

Yes, jumps. Reno was a three-foot horse, maybe three-three, whenever Meredith decided that Sarah was ready. It was their world, with its own rules. I could stop looking for ways to set Sarah on her own path. We owned one.

In the meantime, pride of ownership had an interesting effect on Sarah. Meredith, watching her go around the ring, picked up her bullhorn and called out, "I like that, Sarah. Very nice. Starchy. Don't lose it."

I laughed. "Starchy?"

Meredith answered without taking her eyes off the riders. "Starchy. Put together. That's how I want her."

23 Revising Ophelia

WE KNEW A GIRL WHO HAD A VERY NICE LIFE. WE'D seen bits of it, since the days when she and Sarah went to toddler art camp together, and it seemed an enviable slice of statistical heaven, with two parents, one sibling, a dog, a cat, a beautiful house, and more money than 98 percent of the population. The girl was a completely acceptable specimen, at the high-strung end of the continuum, the sort of girl whom people described as sensitive. She and her mother were close.

About two months before her thirteenth birthday, a strange thing happened. Every time the kid opened her mouth, whether it was to ask if her mom could stop for a cold drink or pick her up in an hour, the woman turned to the closest witness, raised her arms heavenward, and said, "Can you believe this? She is going to be thirteen. I am going to have a teenage girl in the house. I don't know what I'm going to do."

Judith Rich Harris had an understandable empathy for beleaguered parents, because her theory about the relative importance of peers over parents grew out of her own experience with her two daughters, one sugar and spice and one decidedly not. She knew how it felt to be impotent in the face of emotional turmoil — but the mom with the almost-teen didn't yet have a basket case on her hands. She was suffering in anticipation, and I didn't know what to make of that. I asked Harris, who wondered if perhaps the mom knew something about her daughter that the rest of us did not know — that the girl had been an impossible toddler, or that she saved her most heinous behavior for the privacy of home. The poor woman might have had cause for anxiety. She might be warning potential girlfriends and their parents to watch out.

All possible; we had had an occasional glimpse of the girl in unhappy mode, and it was not a pretty sight. Still, she winced every time her mother mentioned her pending birthday. It seemed like the negative advertising was only going to make matters worse.

I wondered how I would feel if Larry's response to my every move were to complain about how old I was and then to seek pity from our friends. I would ask him to hand me the oven mitt, and he would tell our dinner guests that perimenopause had made me impatient, sharp-tongued, critical, and rigid, and he had no idea how he was going to survive this loose-cannon stage of my life. I knew how I would feel — homicidal. I imagined that the girl whose birthday was coming might be having similarly hostile feelings toward her mother.

SCHOOL ENDED a week after Reno moved in, and the most remarkable thing about it was the absence of high drama in the lives of the seventh graders. Yes, there had been an assortment of school infractions. One girl poured a carbonated beverage through the grating of another girl's locker and insisted, on questioning, that she had been provoked by her victim's insults. Two girls may or may not have absconded with a pencil case from the lost and found, and they were suspended for a week. A science lab partner let down her friends by announcing late on a Sunday afternoon that no, she had not completed her part of the project and no, she couldn't find a parent to drive her across town for a planned study date.

Girls flunked tests and wondered how anyone could eat macaroni and cheese and still hope to keep her figure. They sent instant messages to each other and to boys while they were supposed to be finishing their algebra assignment. They snapped at their mothers one minute and professed undying affection the next. The tectonic plates of friendship continued to shift, as they had since the day Sarah switched lunch tables.

As for the older girls, they griped about college applications and test scores and advanced placement requirements and the elusive perfect prom dress. They got turned down by the only school they wanted to go to, and a week later they proudly wore sweatshirts from other schools that were going to be just as grand. One girl was expelled for cheating. One girl, who had defied even institutional efforts to get her to eat, stopped coming to school. The rest of the seniors pushed against what was about to become their past and waited for it to give way. They got ready to leave home.

Life was not without its squabbles, but for the most part they were just that — the kind of tension that inevitably accompanied change, whether it was a daughter growing up, an elderly parent deciding to remarry, or a husband announcing that corporate law no longer held the allure that fly-fishing did.

The consensus, among the front-row moms, was that life was pretty good, which meant that we were either wildly out of sync with the times or capable of self-deception on a global scale, or both. Just as Sarah and her friends prepared to downshift from highly responsible to carefree, to trade their highlighters for sunscreen, a spate of books hit the stores, each one focused on the dreadful fix that was female adolescence. The titles alone were enough to keep us up nights:

Most prominent among them was *Queen Bees and Wannabes: Helping Your Daughter Survive Cliques, Gossip, Boyfriends and Other Realities of Adolescence,* Rosalind Wiseman's book about "helping your daughter make it alive out of junior high," according to the book jacket.

Fast Girls: Teenage Tribes and the Myth of the Slut followed an earlier title, *Slut! Growing Up Female with a Bad Reputation.*

Odd Girl Out: The Hidden Culture of Aggression in Girls looked at bullying and its victims.

The Secret Lives of Girls: What Good Girls Really Do — Sex Play, Aggression, and Their Guilt, a book I'd managed to miss a year earlier, was now out in paperback. It turned out to be a fairly positive appraisal of how girls navigated adolescence, but any happy message got lost, given the provocative title and the popular predisposition to girl bashing.

Most of these stories were told by women who were too young to have teenage daughters themselves, some of whom had just climbed to solid ground after their own adolescence, the memory of swamp life still fresh in their minds. Several of the books were prompted by an author's painful personal experience; like any strife-worn survivor, she wanted us to understand, in perfervid detail, exactly what kind of hell adolescence was. A group of well-intentioned women had set out to address all the "-ions": depression, aggression, sexual alienation, isolation, degradation, humiliation, and on into the emotional night. And yet a coincidence of timing had caused a terrible synergy: Taken alone, each book was a cautionary tale; taken together, they sounded an alarm. It seemed that everything about our girls was a mess.

I bought every last book, stacked them on the bedside table like armor against an attack, and started to work my way through them. Having witnessed a sea change in motherhood in my lifetime, I was, with my peers, a sitting duck for advice books. Reality had shifted since we were children, which made us vulnerable to suggestion and keen on self-improvement. And so a strange thing happened: Like a medical student who develops the symptoms she reads about, I read about bad girls and became convinced that I had one and had missed all the signs.

I saw sinister motive where I used to see nothing more than a bad day. I suspected that happiness was merely the lull before the next storm or, worse, a net of lies. I had an acute case of induced self-doubt — and it would have been possible, right then and there, to lose my way. Before the advice books, Phyllis and I had talked about how the girls had drifted apart again, Julia with her instant messages and her "crew," Sarah with her horse and a new best friend. Now I pored over recent history and wondered if we had seen it all wrong: Was there a pecking order, a terrible cruelty, behind the fact that they hung out together less than they used to?

Not according to *Newsweek,* which attempted to rebut the bad-girl books with a cover article, "Meet the Gamma Girls," about girls who put appearance and popularity in the proper perspective, girls who were too busy playing soccer and protecting their virginity to worry about the amorphous notion of cool. William Damon, director of the Stanford University Center on Adolescence, insisted that these girls were the norm. The new books, he said, "go way beyond what we have data on. They're playing to stereotypes."

We could rest reassured, even if our necks hurt from the whiplash: *Newsweek* had put the "current media flurry" about troubled teen girls in its place. Most girls were not the stuff of nightmares. Most girls were greater than great.

I wondered what it must feel like to wake up every morning knowing that half the adult population considers you a monster, while the other half idolizes you as the best girl in the world. Grown-ups can't handle it. If your boss or spouse thinks you are a monster, you likely get fired, divorced, or ignored; if either one worships the ground you walk on, you have to spend an awful lot of energy living up to that saintly image. And yet we enthusiastically set about categorizing our daughters at one extreme or the other.

Either way, a girl didn't have much wiggle room. We treated her as product, as surely as if she had come off an assembly line. The defective ones had to be fixed, and the perfect ones had to stay perfect. There was no talk of process. We were all about results.

IF GIRLS WERE SOCIETY'S VICTIMS ten years ago, now they were portrayed as perpetrators of all manner of bad behavior; the damaged self-esteem that had first won our attention and sympathy had mutated into verbal, sexual, and physical aggression. Rosalind Wiseman, whose *Queen Bees* led the march to the best-seller list, had intended to provide parents and daughters with better tools for communication, but she feared, in the avalanche of bad-girl publicity, that she had unintentionally contributed to a fundamental misunderstanding.

"Girls are understandably pissed off," she said, "at adults who pathologize them."

She was uncomfortable with the way that books like hers were used as evidence that teenage girls are a mess. "The press really liked the queen bee stuff," said Wiseman, "and it's a starting place for discussions, but some girls get very uncomfortable with it. They say, 'Don't box us in; that's not everybody.' Nobody likes labels, certainly not teenagers, nor do they like the assumption adults make that they know what's going on in a girl's life. These girls have to battle assumptions that they don't buy into themselves."

Lyn Brown was dismayed, but not surprised, at the latest wave of bad-girl sentiment. What it missed, as far as she was concerned, was the source of girls' aggression: She found that girls often got angry because they were fed up with being treated like girls, and they rebelled at the idea that neurosis was a secondary sexual characteristic. They were tired of what Brown called the "double standard" of teen behavior — that boys got compassion and concern and girls, too often, got impatience. The titles of the books on the self-help shelf gave an indication of the collective attitude: We could read about sluts and odd girls, but we never saw the male equivalent on the best-seller list, something like *Bad Boys: Pimps, Dickheads, and Thugs,* because no one would insult boys that way.

As for all the in-fighting among adolescent girls, Brown dismissed the notion that they are hardwired to be vicious to each other. One of the reasons girls fight so much among themselves, she said, is because the rest of us still regard them as provisional citizens. For all their progress on the athletic field and in school, they lack social status. The best way to insult a teenage boy is to say that he is in any way like a girl, not because of the gay implications, but because girls just aren't as cool as boys are. Adults and adolescent boys and sweet innocent children sit higher in the pecking order than adolescent girls do — so the girls take their frustrations out on the only acceptable target, which is each other. In a way, Brown had come to agree with her one-time critic, Linda Kerber: For teenage girls, the personal is political.

Judith Rich Harris simply refused to believe the latest dire dispatches from the front, despite her own experience with her younger daughter. Adolescents can be impossible; she knew that firsthand. Parents can memorize and deliver every single piece of new advice and not make a dent if their daughter chooses not to listen to them. Still, Harris insisted on a grudging optimism. Most girls, she said, simply do not fit the current profile. And she confessed to me one bit of information that did not make it into her book but that alters the equation: Girls have different levels of vulnerability to peer pressure. Not every one of them rushes to do whatever the crowd does.

"Some girls" are a problem, she said, and that was as far as she was prepared to go. Some girls, on the other hand, have the strength to resist bad influences. "It's only the troubled ones," she said, "who get all the attention."

We have managed to marginalize teenage girls, in the great tradition of stereotyping outsiders who frighten us. I remember squirming in my chair when my ninth-grade English class discussed Shylock, that moneygrubbing Jew, and I imagine that a girl today might feel just as awkward about a public perception that boils down to "sluts in short skirts," as a friend of mine put it.

As long as parents set their daughters at arm's length, the girls have only two options. They can try to assimilate: The girl who strives for perfection in mind and body practices an obedient deviance in the hope that she can escape her social caste and make peace in her family by becoming too good to be true. Or they can rebel and confirm everyone's preconceived notion that they are unworthy of our attentions. There is a third alternative, but it requires the adults' cooperation and effort. We can denounce the prevailing media cliché as just that, beat it down with statistics and faith until it gives way. We can give a girl a break. We seem in no great hurry to do so.

If I were a teenage girl, I'd be furious.

24

Unbridled Happiness

HAIRCUT, SPOUSE, PAIR OF BLUE JEANS: NOTHING IS THE same broken in as it is brand-new. A month of summer with Reno and the honeymoon was decidedly over. He would not hold still to take the bit in his mouth. All he had to do was jerk his head up and he was out of our reach. He pulled that trick over and over and over again. He'd take the bit from people who had spent more time around horses but never from the people who fed and clothed and housed him. Never from the people who bought him brand-new shoes every six weeks and forked the manure out of his stall.

Ungrateful teenagers had nothing on this horse. I swore I could hear him snicker every time we walked toward him. His behavior was a fundamental obstacle: no bit, no bridle, no ride. In retrospect, getting Sarah to practice the piano had been easy.

I felt a visceral urge to walk away from all of this. Let the horse wander up to Sunset Boulevard and thumb a ride home with a film executive and her family. Mrs. Dietz was fed up: with herself for being blind to the realities of horse ownership, with Larry for going along with this cockamamie idea, with Sarah for not being six feet tall, a hundred and eighty formidable pounds. With Reno, for betraying our trust.

It was okay as long as someone else was around, because the humiliation of asking for help was far easier to tolerate than the pain in my shoulder when Reno tried to yank my arm out of its socket. I was not above begging, though I tried to do it only when Meredith was not there to hear me. She was as disappointed in us as we were in the horse. She considered us wimps.

On one midsummer Sunday, the canyon was deserted. It was up to Sarah and me. We rubbed sugar on the bit. Sarah stood on the mounting block and dangled the bridle in front of Reno's head so that the bit was just inches away from his mouth. I stuck my thumb in the space between Reno's clenched front and back teeth and tickled the roof of his mouth, and with my other hand I raised the bit. Nothing happened. I tried again.

"Don't press the bit against his teeth," said Sarah. "He doesn't like that."

After twenty desperate minutes at the stall, Sarah suggested that we walk him up to the ring in his halter, and then we could try again.

"Maybe he'll be happier where there's more space," she said.

Gee, I sure hoped so, because his happiness was paramount in my life.

I was in thrall to a mammal with a brain the size of a walnut or a pea, depending on whom you asked, a handsome airhead who wanted his space. If that was how I wanted to spend my time, I could have married a male model or a gumball heir. I had a psychology professor in college who insisted that all anger was really a cover for a more genuine, and vulnerable, sorrow, but I doubted the horse would empathize if I confessed that I felt sad about the quality of our relationship.

We walked down the street to the riding rings, slipped the reins up over Reno's neck, unbuckled the halter, gently held the bit in front of his teeth, and failed. Again and again and again. I saw Sarah's ride disappearing, which meant that Reno would be more of a crank tomorrow. I saw my ride disappearing, since Sarah always invited me to ride after she'd worn him out enough to make me feel safe. Worst of all, I saw no solution to the problem. Meredith was big on the mouth tickle, but clearly Reno had not read that section in the instruction manual.

"Okay," I said to Sarah. "You stand on one side, I'll stand on the other, and we'll try it one more time."

She whispered lies to him about what a great horse he was, I raised the bit with one hand and tickled the roof of his mouth with the other, and just like that, as though we had never had a problem before, the big teeth parted and we had a horse wearing a bridle.

Sarah did a little victory dance while I hastily buckled all the straps in place, and then we reviewed the specifics of our conquest — the quality of the tickle, the exact placement of the bit, the speed with which we looped the bridle over his ears. We complimented each other on our remarkable calm — and then Sarah confessed that she had expected me to give up.

"There was one minute there, where I thought you were going to put the halter back on and walk up the street," she said. "I could feel you getting angry."

"I felt the same way about you," I said. If Larry had been with us, he would have done the little pantomime he'd worked up, of an apple not falling far from the tree.

But we did not lose our tempers, and that, not the bridle, was the victory. We did not snipe at each other, not a syllable, and we did not give up, and in my euphoria I was sure that all of this boded well for the future. If we could get the bridle on Reno, we could handle anything, even the next five years of Sarah's life.

Doomed to failure one minute, able to leap tall buildings in a single bound the next. Girls were not the only ones who had mood swings during their adolescence.

"We are the bridle team," Sarah crowed.

I was giddy. "And when we go to the Vera Wang sale," I said, "we can be the bridal team."

"It'll go on forever," Sarah cried. "The bridle team and the bridal team."

It would not go on forever. Or it would, but not like this. There would come a day, before the summer ended, when I dropped her off at the stall and she tacked up Reno for her lesson, alone. There would be days when she fairly flew out of the car to catch up with a friend who was getting ready to ride, dismissing me with a backward wave and half a distracted smile.

One afternoon, after I had asked too many questions about aspects of riding that were none of my business, she slid her imperious self into the passenger seat and stared out the window as I drove home.

"I am going to be blunt," she said. Girls her age tried on phrases like shoes, to see what showed them off to advantage, and every now and then they said something that sounded three sizes too big. It got my attention.

"I'm listening."

"You do not have to do as many things for me as you did a couple of years ago," she said, "when I was helpless."

I lurched the car over to the curb with a strength of purpose that surprised both of us.

"Sarah," I said, "you may have needed help with more things a few years ago, but I never thought of you as helpless. I *never* thought of you as helpless."

NO, SUNDAY AFTERNOON with a bridled horse, alone, us two, would not last very long, nor was it supposed to. But that day, Sarah had twisted her sea of wheat hair up under her helmet, and I had forgotten to think ahead. All I knew was that the horse had the bit in his mouth, we had the ring to ourselves, and we were ready, this laughing girl and I, to ride.

Out of My Head

NOT DAWN, NOT YET. WE WALKED RENO TO THE HORSE trailer in the dark, and then we drove along three freeways, the backseat full of leather tack and brushes and the trunk full of alfalfa hay. Sarah tried not to doze off and occasionally failed.

Four mornings each year, I got to see the sun come up, so that Sarah could get to the school-league horse show on time. I hated getting out of bed that early, but once I did, I loved being awake in the dark. We headed for the Los Angeles Equestrian Center, which had become a little village overnight, as though it were a movie set dressed for the day's shoot. Hundreds of people and a couple hundred horses appeared, were very busy for twelve hours, and disappeared. Hope, diligence, and a great deal of drama culminated in disappointment or reward, some of which had nothing to do with ability, just like in the real world. We were home in time for dinner.

This was the first show of Sarah's eighth-grade season, and Reno's debut; she was bursting with pride, but her four classes were not until the end of the day. There was little to do except pet his nose and watch the other girls go around. Larry came out a bit later, so we broke out the sandwiches and cookies we'd brought for lunch, and then we waited some more. As the other classes ran long, the end of the day got further and further away.

By the time it was Sarah's turn, the sun was heading for the hilltops, and its light had turned to a silvery peach. Like the barn-sour horses of my youth, Larry and I were starting to think of home.

Not Sarah. She rode Reno over to the warm-up ring as though she had not been up since daybreak and waiting ever since. I leaned against the fence to watch them, and all of a sudden I remembered when she was three, dressed in a red leotard and wings for a dance recital, and the teacher called the kids to the center of the floor. Sarah had caught sight of herself in the mirror, and she turned and cried out to me.

"Oh, Mommy," she said, enraptured with the wonderfulness of being her, "look how beautiful I am."

She came into the warm-up ring like that, at least to me, although anyone else would have seen just another kid walking around on a big brown horse. I took a photograph that day that is my favorite, of the hundreds I would take of girl and horse. They were coming around a corner at the canter, and for a split second they balanced on Reno's left front leg. The sun cut steel lines on Sarah's boot and Reno's flank, in the instant before the motion was resolved, before he came down to earth and took another step. I love that picture out of all proportion; there are prettier photographs, but that is the one I like the best. If it were music, it would be the grace note. It was anticipation.

She cantered to the far end of the warm-up ring, and then she turned again and came straight toward me, smiling. I could not speak, so I raised my hand to the base of my throat and patted my chest, up and down, up and down, to the beat of my heart.

As she rode past, the girl who once believed in an Italian bilingual writing bear laughed and said, "Mom, it's only a horse show."

I shook my head. It had nothing at all to do with ribbons and judges. Dust, and waiting, and being out of my natural habitat, and her joy, had accomplished what I, alone, could not: My ch'i was in my feet — inside my scuffed and hard-toed boots — and not in my head. The acupuncturist who had warned that my mind was working overtime would have been impressed. I was incapable of rational thought.

I refused to consider what came next, not even the immediate question of whether we would be able to nudge Reno into the wash rack a half hour from now. It was that parallel track, the endless strategy meeting, that turned children into commodities and made adolescence a protracted fight for control of the company. Nobody was immune: We would talk about grades and friendship and extracurricular activities, and we would joke about how useless horseback riding looked on a college application. We would evaluate and compare and agonize, along with everyone else.

Not now.

Sarah took one more lap around the warm-up ring, arriving at the gate just as it was her turn to go in. She entered the ring without stopping, without time for a glance back or for the kiss I had intended to send in her direction. When the announcer read out her name and number, she sat up just a bit straighter. Then she cantered away from me at an angle, across the ring.

Starchy, I thought to myself.

Nobody's girl but her own.

EPILOGUE

THE ARCHAEOLOGICAL DIG THAT IS SARAH'S BEDROOM tells the whole story. In the corner behind the door, a congealed glob of stuffed animals. The ones at the bottom of the wooden toy crib had not seen daylight in years, but they were protected from being discarded by the slightly more popular animals that sat on top of them. A random paw or plastic nose stuck out from between the ribs of the crib, but it was hard to tell where the dog in the pink hat left off and the bear with the button eyes began.

Next to them, freestanding, the bigger and more memorable animals — the kangaroo with a baby in her pocket, the gorilla that dwarfed Sarah when it first arrived, the big purple walrus puppet that Harry brought her for her first birthday.

That was the most ancient section of the site. On the other side of the doorway, the bookshelves. The picture books were packed away in the closet now, replaced by what the elementary school librarians called chapter books, plus horse magazines and the occasional title borrowed from our shelves, horizontal stacks on top of vertical ones. It looked as though they might topple at any moment, but Sarah refused to give up a single one, on the off chance that tomorrow she might yearn to reread it.

The venetian blinds no longer opened because they were covered with horse show ribbons, hung in descending order around the room, and there was talk of stringing a wire across the top of the one blank wall to hold the ones she had not yet won.

The chair held sedimentary layers of clothing — horse clothes on the left arm, school clothes on the right, pajama pants, jeans that no longer fit, scarves. Dirty socks burrowed inside shoes, to be discovered only on the day when Sarah realized there were no clean ones left in her drawer.

Ah, but the top of the dresser was the treasure trove: six glass horses, the biggest an inch tall, that our Seattle friends brought back from Mexico; an inch-long pewter hedgehog from Florence; a row of horses that included a survivor from my collection, his tail and part of one leg missing; a photo Sarah took of Larry and me; little cardboard boxes of jewelry that wouldn't fit into the big jewelry box; and way at the end, against the wall, a two-foot-tall carousel she'd built for a science project, with painted clay horses. We didn't have the technology to make them go up and down, but they did spin when she turned the top by hand.

It was a room crammed with life, or a mess, depending on your point of view. I made occasional noises about cleaning it up, but it was her room, after all, so we settled on a compromise: If anyone was coming over who might conceivably want to enter her room, she had to clean off the chair and make the bed so that a visitor could sit down without impaling herself on a zipper. I remembered what a family therapist had said at some school meeting: If a house with children was too clean, somebody wasn't having a good time. I chose not to solicit conflicting opinions.

Sarah turned thirteen right after that first school-league show with Reno, in October of eighth grade, and we threw her a little surprise party, just the front-row families, because she could not figure out which other girls she wanted to invite or what to do to make sure they all had a good time. To mark her official status as a teenager, I asked each girl to compose a list of thirteen great things about Sarah, which they recited after dinner.

Fourteen, and ninth grade, was something else again: When we offered to take eight of her friends to a concert, she came up with a list of names right away. They blew past me at the door as though I were a support beam, and they descended on Sarah, who had finally graduated from the children's department and had a new skirt to prove it.

"Where'd you get that skirt?" demanded one girl I'd never met.

"I want to borrow that skirt," said another.

"I'm going to *steal* that skirt," said Emily. "Give it to me!"

"That is so cool," said yet another stranger.

There was just enough time for dinner before we left, so they filled their plates and sat down at the dining room table, nine nicely dressed girls eating like very polite wolves. They bused their own plates when they were done, without being asked. They said thank you for dinner before we piled into the cars. There was one fairly short skirt and one visible navel among them.

Larry and I ate standing at the kitchen counter, because even if there had been room for us at the table, there wasn't room for us at the table.

When we got to the theater, he pulled me aside. "One of them already has her driver's permit," he whispered, his voice rising in disbelief, "and she was talking about driving a car."

PARENTS AGE IN DISTINCT STAGES, in a way that childless people do not. Mrs. Dietz was only the beginning of my transformation from essential spiritual guide to teenager's mom. Harry and Judith, my childless control group, continued to get older a year at a time, in a fluid rush of unexpected, unplanned events. The only highway sign worth noticing in their spontaneous lives was the transition from one decade into the next, which faded from view as soon as the day passed.

But Karen had become Mrs. Dietz, who had a teenage daughter. Last time I blinked, I was watching Sarah struggle with her stirrups at her first Meredith lesson. Now I sat in the same spot on the bleachers, as Sarah and another girl walked their horses around, chatting a mile a minute. When they got within earshot of me, I heard Sarah say, "Let's trot."

So they trotted past me, past earshot, and then they slowed to a walk, and resumed their conversation.

I was not concerned about the content of the conversation, since the closest the canyon girls came to sustained venom would probably be to criticize the way so-and-so jumped her horse. Experts might smile at the level of self-deception in that statement, but experts needed to factor in the horse. The issue of teenage malice was moot in the canyon, beyond the occasional snide comment or a reluctance to ride around with one girl instead of another. I'm not saying that the girls all loved one another, because they didn't — just that there was little time to waste on intramural spats. Meredith insisted on a level of cooperation that made it almost impossible to nurse a grudge. Three times a week, the girls had to set the jumps for the group lesson, occasionally trade horses, and manage not to crash into each other, all of which required a decent rapport.

I didn't fret about the elided conversation. What got my attention was the simple need to exclude me, even if it was from a dialogue that did not require secrecy. Mrs. Dietz was not part of the modern universe. She was Mom.

THE NEXT AFTERNOON, I was out in the cold again — left in the waiting room at our pediatrician's office, with nothing to read but baby magazines. Doctor Jim had a teen privacy policy: Thirteen was the last time he allowed a parent to accompany a child into the exam room. At fourteen his patients came in alone, in case there was anything they wanted to talk to him about in confidence. I would be in the way.

Not me personally; nobody left me out because I was a bad person. They left me out because I was Mrs. Dietz, and this was the moment I was supposed to step to the side. I was appropriately peripheral. So I read about breast-feeding and watched a mother teach her daughter how to punch the buttons on the waiting-room juke box, as some mother I didn't notice must have watched me teach Sarah a decade ago.

When Dr. Jim came out to get me, he had a funny look on his face — a little awe, a little empathy. He put a hand on my shoulder and guided me toward his office.

"I don't get it," he said. "When, exactly, did she grow up?"

"If I'm barefoot and she has her riding boots on, she can look me in the eye," I said. "And I don't think I can pick her up anymore."

He wasn't talking about her height. I confessed that lately I had been excused from a growing number of activities, always with great courtesy on Sarah's part: I did not need to sit through the entire riding lesson if I wanted to take a walk; I did not need to stay downstairs if I wanted to go upstairs to read the paper in bed while she finished her homework; I could stay home with Dad while she went to the choral concert with Aviva and slept over at her house.

I was not a fool. I knew that in truth, Sarah might not want me around, but I played along and answered just as politely that I appreciated her being so considerate. I no longer had to concern myself with promoting Sarah's independence; she had taken over the job. At least she gave some thought to what I might do with my free time, instead of telling me to get lost.

I do not mean to imply that she was one of those perfect gamma girls. She was capable of finding fault with almost anything, from my enthusiasm for dental floss to the frequency with which I served fish for dinner. At a low point in Reno's career, she demanded that I not speak to her before she went into the ring and that I not make faces when she was riding, whatever that meant. She seemed to want a mute on Botox for a mother. She seemed to think I was capable of villainous telepathy with a horse. I told her she was taking her frustration out on me, and I reminded her that she had a wildly supportive mother, in the pantheon of horse moms. I left it at that because it wasn't a fight worth picking. She got over it.

I did take the occasional walk during a lesson, and once I failed to come back in time to help her switch bridles for jumping. Sarah proudly informed me that Meredith said she was even faster when she did it by herself, and she was so pleased that I saw, just for an instant, how complicated it is to grow up. We forget. At any given moment, there is so much going on. She wanted not to need me, she wanted always to need me, she felt pleased and guilty, all in the time it now took to get the bit in his mouth, which, these days, was no time at all.

We had no choice about what was happening, but it seemed to me that we had a profound choice about how it happened, and I was determined to think the best of her unless I had cold evidence to the contrary.

THE FOURTEENTH-BIRTHDAY GIRLS did what girls do at concerts — they shrieked, they applauded, they hugged each other, they sat on the edge of their seats. Judith was there with her digital camera, so she took a group photo. It was irrefutable evidence: not a little girl in the group; they faced the camera straight on, smiling like bandits with their arms around each other.

Larry e-mailed the photo to a bunch of his friends so that they could be as amazed as he was at how quickly Sarah had grown. He made sure to identify which one she was, in case people no longer recognized her.

Annette was the first one to write back. She questioned Larry's description of who was who, "because that means the adult beauty to the right is Sarah, which I know to be impossible, because Sarah is a darling little girl. Isn't she??????? WHAT'S HAPPENED????????"

She signed it, "Nonplussed, Annette."

Indeed.

I wrote back to Annette and told her that she was absolutely right. That was not Sarah in the photograph — or rather, it was not all of Sarah.

"I think of Sarah," I wrote, "as a darling little girl in an adult-beauty costume."

I HAVE A SET of seven small photographs that I took years before, when Sarah was five, maybe six. She had gotten out of the shower and put on a somewhat asymmetrical pair of new white flannel pajamas, which I'd made for her, clumsily, because she coveted mine and no store carried them in her size. For the first time, I'd wrapped a towel around her wet hair, like a turban, to keep it from soaking through the pajama top. She was transformed by her new costume. She began a strange little dance, a series of poses, really, with her arms and legs at odd angles and her mouth set in a mysterious smile. She looked straight through me.

We never kept the camera upstairs, but that night it was within reach for no good reason. I grabbed it and started taking pictures, and she kept dancing until she got to her final pose — her right hand under her chin, fingers pointing out, and her left hand holding up her left leg by her toes.

These are my travel photos — little Sarah in her pajamas, bigger Sarah cantering Reno, teenage Sarah with her pals. They are souvenirs of all the places we've been, the unexpected jaunts we have taken that required only the willingness to go. I am larger than my own life, thanks to her, and if things ever get rough, I have the pictures to remind me of that. I have little of the kind of faith that propped up cultures, but I have come to believe in abiding moments of grace.

I put the pajama photos in a frame together, in sequence. They hang on the wall in my office, across from my desk. I used to try to figure out where that dance came from, but there is no way to know. After a while I stopped guessing. I look at the pictures every now and then: Sarah is always here, Sarah is always leaving, and so far, we are just fine.

ACKNOWLEDGMENTS

A quartet of passionate moms enabled me to write this book. I am forever grateful to my agent, Lynn Nesbit, for not expecting me to write the same kind of book I always write, and to Sarah Crichton for taking a chance on a journalist who wasn't being a journalist. Editor Deborah Baker stepped in with provocative questions. And then came editor Pat Strachan, a fellow midwesterner who grew up liking horses; it was a great joy to work with her.

My thanks as well to Richard Morris at Janklow & Nesbit, to Michael Pietsch, Sophie Cottrell, Heather Rizzo, and Peggy Freudenthal at Little, Brown, to Camille McDuffie and Lynn Goldberg, and to Brian Siberell. Tina Simms and Helen Atsma made sure that everything got done.

Lyn Mikel Brown, Judith Rich Harris, and Rosalind Wiseman provided context for my personal observations, and I appreciate the time they took to talk about adolescent girls. Sarah Blackwill and Mary Trahan helped to collect additional research.

The denizens of Sullivan Canyon — particularly the members of Toyon Farm — taught me what little I know about horses, and much more about community, and I thank every dirty, dusty one of them for making us part of the crowd.

Carolyn See makes lunch worth eating and the writer's life worth living. Ginger Curwen has the same effect at dinner. I am lucky to have them as friends.

I am grateful for the opportunity to reprint a few of the poems that appeared in John Espey's *Empty Box Haiku.*

Great thanks to early readers Harry Shearer, who dotes on my daughter, and William Whitworth, who dotes on his own. Judith Owen married into the role of godmother and does a splendid job. Patty Williams truly does steal one's soul when she takes a photograph — but she catches it so gently that I never mind. Marcie Rothman and Kathy Rich saved me by not wanting to talk about the book all the time. Annette Duffy Odell supplied inspiration without even trying.

I'm grateful to the front-row families — Vicky, Hummie, Sarah, and Jessi; Jo Ann, Jay, and Aviva; Lori, Roy, Cara, and Emily; Phyllis, Raphe, Julia, and Anna — for being themselves. Thanks to all the seder families for showing up every year.

Thanks to my real family, a small but select group: to my mother, Norma Rae; my sister, Lori; and my niece and nephew, Lesly and Josh. And a nod to my father, Ira, who still lives in our hearts.

Larry Dietz gave up great restaurants and learned how to tack up a horse, and he caved in on the dog he swore he'd never have again because our daughter, Sarah, wanted one. He has become a family man; I thank him for traveling for so long without a road map.

There is an unwritten rule that says not to include in the acknowledgments the person to whom a book is dedicated. I choose to ignore it. I thank Sarah for teaching me everything I didn't know before.

ABOUT THE AUTHOR

Karen Stabiner's previous books include *All Girls, Single-Sex Education and Why It Matters,* and *To Dance with the Devil: The New War on Breast Cancer,* a *New York Times* Notable Book. Her work has appeared in the *Los Angeles Times, The New Yorker,* the *New York Times, O, Vogue,* and many other periodicals. Stabiner lives in Santa Monica, California, with her husband and their daughter.